Magic's Touch

Even as a fierce competitor,
I try to find time for a smile.

Magic's Touch

*Earvin "Magic" Johnson, Jr.
and Roy S. Johnson*

ADDISON-WESLEY PUBLISHING COMPANY, INC.

*Reading, Massachusetts ● Menlo Park, California ● New York
Don Mills, Ontario ● Wokingham, England ● Amsterdam ● Bonn
Sydney ● Singapore ● Tokyo ● Madrid ● San Juan*

Photo Credits

The photograph that appears on page 30 was provided courtesy of Michigan State University Sports Information.

All other photographs were provided by NBA Photos: Andrew D. Bernstein, v, xxx, 6, 10, 13, 17, 20, 24, 34, 38, 40, 42, 47, 50, 52, 56, 60, 64, 66, 68, 72, 75, 79, 81, 83, 88, 91, 96, 100, 102, 108, 113, 117, 120, 122, 123, 126, 130, 134, 138, 141, 146, 150, 152, 154, 158, 163, 166, 169, 170, 174, 190, 194, 201, 203, 216, 222, 224, 225, 228, 231, 234; Nathaniel Butler, 27, 36, 77, 85; Al Gonzalez, 132, 156, 182, 184; Steve W. Grayson, 93; Jon Soohoo, 138, 143.

Library of Congress Cataloging-in-Publication Data

Johnson, Earvin, 1959–
   Magic's touch / Earvin "Magic" Johnson, Jr., and Roy S. Johnson.
      p.   cm.
   ISBN 0-201-51794-9
   1. Johnson, Earvin, 1959– .   2. Basketball players—United
States—Biography.   3. Los Angeles Lakers (Basketball team)
I. Johnson, Roy S. II. Title.
GV884.J63A3 1989
796.323′092—dc20
[B]   89-17494

Cover design: Mike Stromberg
Text design: Joy Dickinson/Editorial Design
Illustration: John A. Lytle
Production: Michael Bass & Associates
Composition: Set in 11 point ITC Garamond Book
   by Bookends Typesetting, Ashland, Oregon

ABCDEFGHIJ-DO-89
First printing, August 1989

TO MOM AND DAD, CHRISTINE AND EARVIN.

—*E.J., Jr.*

TO BIG ROY. I MISS YOU.

—*R.S.J.*

Contents

Acknowledgments

To all of my coaches: Jim Dart, Lewis Brockhaus, Dick Rosecran, George Fox, Jud Heathcote, Jack McKinney, Paul Westhead, and Pat Riley.

E.J., Jr.

Any book of this sort requires cooperation, tolerance, understanding, commitment, and encouragement. For providing me with those gifts at a time when I needed them most, I would like to thank my family, including my mother, Ida Mae Jenkis, and cousin Janice, who listened; my agent, Michael Carlisle, who patiently pieced the puzzle together; my editors at *The Atlanta Constitution* and *Sports Illustrated,* Vam McKenzie and Mark Mulvoy, who tolerated my harried schedule; to Sandy Padwe, who's been encouraging me for more than ten years; to Langston Hughes and Frederick Douglass, my inspiration; and to Norman, who only cared that I came home in time for a walk.

R.S.J.

I thought I'd seen it all when it came to basketball—every style, every size and shape player there was. I'd been involved with the sport as an observer, player, or coach for years, beginning with my own days as a young boy growing up and playing in the hills of West Virginia, through four years at the University of West Virginia and fourteen seasons in the National Basketball Association, then as an NBA head coach and general manager. I'd seen shorter-than-average centers, taller-than-average guards, and players with more talent than you might have thought was possible. I'd played against and been teammates with guys like Oscar Robertson, Bill Russell, and Wilt Chamberlain, three of the best players who ever lived.

And then I saw Magic Johnson.

He was still a freshman at Michigan State when I first saw him play. The Spartans were on television, and I remember that almost immediately something about him struck me as being very odd, almost awkward. I suddenly found myself staring at the screen in amazement. Here was this 6'-9" kid with a big man's body, well over 200 pounds, playing what was essentially a little man's game. He was the size of most college centers, but he was playing point guard for his team. He was the floor leader, calling all the plays and moving everybody around the floor like an orchestra leader. He was handling the ball like a six-footer, like it was an extension of his hand. He was absolutely in complete command. And he was making the kind of moves I'd never seen from a player his size. He was dribbling the length of the floor, looking one way and passing another. He was hitting every open man, making all the right decisions. Basically, he was controlling the entire game, touching the ball on every Michigan State possession. He was their unmistakable leader. Before anything could happen, it had to go through Magic, a 6'–9" point guard. I was astounded.

Even after Magic led Michigan State to the national title, I wasn't convinced that Magic would be able to play his game in the NBA, where the players are bigger, stronger, quicker, and more talented than the average college player. The most challenging part of my job as the Los Angeles Lakers' general manager is to keep the team stocked with talented players who complement each other. One way to accomplish that is through the college draft, so scouting college players takes up most of my time. One of the hardest judgments to make is whether a successful player will be able to achieve similar results in the NBA. Not even all-Americans have a lock on success. The game is littered with big-name "busts," Can't-Miss Kids who missed the target completely. Every general manager, including myself, has at least one name on his draft résumé that he would just as soon erase. So it was only natural that I wondered if Magic, a 6'–9" point guard, would be able to pull off those same stunts in the pros. There had been tall guards in the NBA, guys like George (The Iceman) Gervin and, of course, Oscar Robertson. But the league had never seen a 6'–9" point guard. I figured Magic would become a power forward. He was the perfect size, and he had a solid, muscular build. Even so, after watching him play point guard for two seasons in college, I didn't know if he could play with his back to the basket like a traditional low-post player, whether he could use his keen vision and uncanny feel for the game in a position where he would be subjected to more physical resistance. Then I had to wonder that if he couldn't make the adjustments would he become frustrated? Would he become just another great college player who met mortality in the NBA? Ten years after the fact, I'm almost embarrassed to admit I had my doubts.

Greatness is one of the most overused words in sports these days. But Magic Johnson is a *truly great* basketball player, one of only three or four in the entire league. There are a lot of guys who are very good, and some are even special, but only a handful of players like Magic—guys like Larry Bird and Michael Jordan—have that special ability to make those around them better. That's one way to define basketball greatness—to be able to use your skills to benefit your teammates. When the Lakers chose Earvin (Magic) Johnson with the first pick of the 1979 college draft, he became the foundation that allowed the team to dominate the next entire decade. The Lakers won five championships—including two straight in the 1987 and 1988 seasons—and reached the NBA finals eight times during the 1980s, Magic's first ten years as a pro and the leader of our team. So our success was no coincidence. I once told a friend that when Earvin Johnson, Jr., was born, he was sprinkled with Magic dust.

Once I became used to the idea of a point guard who was as big as Bill Russell, as smart and creative as Tiny Archibald, and as exciting as Bob Cousy, I began to notice something else that set Magic apart from other college players. In the middle of all these tremendous gifts, there was this tremendous smile. Magic Johnson had an uncommon enthusiasm for the game. When he was play-ing basketball, it seemed like he was having the time of his life. That's something special, something you simply can't teach a player, and it's something that's had a direct impact on Magic's ability to survive the various peaks and valleys of his career. No one will ever forget Magic's opening night in the pros when he leaped into the arms of Kareem Abdul-Jabbar after he hit a skyhook to beat the L.A. Clippers on national television. Kareem is a stoic player during the regular season, all business. So he was stunned when this kid jumped on him like the team had just won the title. No one knew it then, but Magic's enthusiasm would rub off on the whole team and draw the players together. Years later, when Magic was blamed for our losing to the Boston Celtics in the 1984 NBA finals, I was afraid the criticism would devastate him and affect the rest of his career. That it didn't—we won the title the next year—was a reflection of his enthusiasm and his respect for the game. Basketball meant too much to Magic for even a disastrous defeat to douse his love for the game.

An enthusiastic player is also a hard-working player, a player who's committed to the game. A player who truly loves playing basketball, and who isn't in it only for the notoriety and the money, will never stop trying to improve. That's Magic. Already, he's as fundamentally sound as anyone in the league, but he's also an example of the benefits of hard work. No one who has ever watched Magic for a long period of time, no one who has ever played with him, and no one who's ever coached him has questioned his work ethic. At times, I almost think he practices *too* hard. To see the pace he maintains during practices and games is astounding. But the results are evident.

Every day I marvel at how far he's come, how much he's changed and improved his game since his days at Michigan State. He wasn't always a great shooter. Now, he is. He didn't always have lethal moves in the low post. Now, he does. From being a great college player, Magic Johnson has molded himself into a great pro player, one of the best there ever was.

I wasn't alone in wondering if Magic would be able to dominate in the pros like he did in college. There were plenty of general managers who saw this vibrant kid and wondered. That much energy combined with an equal amount of dedication is almost too much to ask for, they said. The prevailing thought was that he wouldn't be able to carry that enthusiasm through the long, grinding NBA season and that when he lost his enthusiasm he'd become discouraged. It never happened. Just watch Magic perform every night. If his body allows him to play at all, he will. He'd rather practice than take a day off. Some guys take practices off if they've got a hangnail. Not Magic. It takes a severe injury to keep him off the floor. In fact, with all the pounding he takes in games, I sometimes have to order him to rest. Of course, he acts like he doesn't hear me. I get more amazed at how hard he practices than by anything I've seen him do in games. Any player will be enthusiastic about the games. Magic is enthusiastic about practice, which has been the key to his improvement.

Such devotion to the game and commitment to an unyielding work ethic have been Magic's trademarks since the day he arrived in Los Angeles. That's why I always laugh when I hear people calling him a flashy player. Nothing can be further from the truth. You don't see him throwing a lot of behind-the-back passes or dribbling between his legs, unless it's necessary. Basically, what you see in Magic is a fundamental player, almost a simplistic player. And as far as most coaches and general managers are concerned, the simpler the better. He has a strong attention to detail, and after most practices he still works on the areas of his game where he might be able to take advantage of his opponent. His ball handling, especially on the break, is impeccable, but no one hurts more about making mistakes than he does. Most of his turnovers have come when the Lakers have a big lead. That's when he tries to do too much, when he maybe becomes an entertainer for the crowd. But you rarely see him make a turnover that hurts the team. And when he does make a mistake, Magic only makes it once.

Different players can teach you different things about the game of basketball. Some can teach you how to shoot with the proper form; others are skillful passers, rebounders, or defensive geniuses. Magic Johnson epitomizes all those skills in one package better than anyone who has ever played the game. And he can teach you one more thing. He can teach you about winning. It's the reason he plays the game, and the reason he's, well, Magic.

INTRODUCTION
Roy S. Johnson

A new day dawned on Lansing, Michigan, as Earvin Johnson, Sr., walked into the room of his youngest son and stirred the child from his deepest sleep. The tall, lanky teenager, known to almost everyone around the neighborhood as "Junior," looked up slowly and rubbed his eyes. It was 7 AM.

"How'd you do last night?" the father asked.

"We won by twenty," the son responded, though still mostly asleep.

"OK, good," the father said. "Now, get up. You've still got to work on the truck. You may be 'Magic' down at the gym, but around here, you're still 'Junior.'"

Such were the Saturday mornings of Magic Johnson's youth, occasions when he was dragged from his quiet slumber, his world of basketball dreams, and thrust into a reality where hard work was the only staple of survival. Earvin Johnson, Sr., was the father of ten children in this working-class neighborhood in suburban Detroit. Their care and feeding was his responsibility and his alone, he often told his son. So he handled two full-time jobs—a 5 PM to 1 AM shift assembling automobiles at the nearby General Motors plant and a one-man (and son) hauling service that picked up rubbish, discarded barrels, bag-filled trash or twigs, bundled branches, and anything else from customers, and completed several other not-so-enviable chores.

"Any garages that used oil," Magic recalls, "we'd come in while the shop was closed, soap down the floor, let it dry, then come back later and wash it down. Sometimes, Dad would go in and scrub the concrete floors after his shift at 2 AM, then come home and get a few hours sleep, wake up to go finish the hauling jobs, take an afternoon nap, then go back to work at the plant while the rest of us were sitting down for dinner. He did that every single day. He *worked*. He used to say, 'I've got ten mouths to feed. Nobody else did this, I did.' That was him."

Long before Earvin (Magic) Johnson led Michigan State to the national collegiate basketball championship, long before he would carry the Los Angeles Lakers to five world championships during his first decade in the NBA, and long before the spring of 1989 when he was named the league's Most Valuable Player for the second time in his stellar career, "Junior" was a high school phenomenon, a basketball legend throughout Michigan. But early on Saturday mornings during the school year and every day in the summer, "Junior" still joined his father along his hauling route, working until basketball practice began at 10 AM. Work and practice were mandatory for Earvin, Jr. So was having a job after practice where he stacked boxes at the corner dairy.

"And yard work? Don't remind me about those kinds of mowers that rolled the blades over the grass, or snow shovels," Magic says. "In the winters, Dad would say, 'Make sure the driveway's clear plus all the walkways. Do Miss George's walkway next door, too.' Then he'd say, 'I'll see you when I get back,' and off he'd go for another job. How could I refuse when *he* was working so hard? If I wanted money to go to the show, he'd say, 'See these want ads over there? That's what they're there for.' And if it was summer, he'd make me take that lawn mower around and cut yards for money. If it was winter, I took the snow shovel and felt like I was clearing the whole neighborhood. But no matter what I did, I never worked as hard as he did."

And there was no such thing as the son testing the father's limits. "You didn't even think about it," says Magic. "My dad didn't stand for that. He'd punish you and didn't care how he did it."

It's near the end of the 1988–89 NBA season—a season that would end in sour disappointments, a hamstring injury in game two of the NBA finals, and a four-game sweep by the Detroit Pistons that ended the Lakers' two-year reign as champions—and Earvin (Magic) Johnson is resting inside another hotel room in another city on the road. In the midst of the conversation and the memories, he paused and smiled. "All those things paid off for me because I see it all so clearly now. I see everything he was trying to teach me. I look for nothing from nobody. Whatever I want, I work for. He kept stressing the importance of school to us because he never got a chance to go himself. He was a man who started his family as a boy, then provided for them as a man. He used to tell me, 'I don't want to see you end up in this factory like I did.'"

He didn't. Instead "Junior" became "Magic," perhaps the greatest point guard of all time, the architect, conductor, and CEO of championship basketball, Lakers-style. Someday, the youngest son will undoubtedly find himself in pro basketball's Hall of Fame in Springfield, Massachusetts. When that day arrives, it would be fitting that one other person also be inducted— Earvin Johnson, Sr.

"He's a big fan, my biggest fan, and the reason I was able to succeed," says Magic. "He taught me about hard work. How important to me was it that he got up and worked *two* jobs every day? Very important because that's the motivation I used from the time I started playing basketball. He taught me that I wasn't going to get anything in basketball or life without working for it. That's why I get so mad when people say I'm just a flamboyant player, a guy who doesn't work hard. Early in my career with the Lakers, that's all I'd hear. I'd get a rebound, run down the court, make the assist, run back on defense, help stop the other team, then start it all over again. All the while I'd be thinking about some of the things people were saying about me, and I would say to myself, 'I guess I'm not really playing hard. I'm just hanging out waiting for the outlet pass so I can run down the floor and make a fancy pass.' I'd just shake my head. What people were saying didn't make any sense at all. Those people didn't know me, and they didn't know my father."

There are many professional athletes in a variety of sports whose skills aren't defined by substance, but camouflaged by flash. Most often, their athletic lives are fleeting, lasting only a few ordinary, insignificant seasons. They dash through our stadiums and arenas like comets across the sky, brilliance unfulfilled. By contrast, Magic Johnson has endured, surviving ten dazzling seasons, nearly three lifetimes for the average athlete. But more than that, he has also established himself as an embodiment of what every athlete aspires to be: a winner.

He's a player whose skills are so refined, so pure, so commanding that they seem to transcend the generations. Magic is a craftsman on the basketball court, an engaging artist to be placed inside an athletic time machine, the vehicle through which we dream of how our current sports heroes might have fared against their peers from another time. It's how we dream of Muhammad Ali inside a ring with Rocky Marciano or of Joe Louis answering the opening bell against Mike Tyson. It's how we imagine Satchel Paige staring down from the mound toward Wade Boggs or Ted Williams toeing the line inside the batter's box against Dwight Gooden. It's how we watch Wayne Gretzky charging down the ice against Bobby Orr, or Boris Becker blasting a serve at Rod Laver, or Carl Lewis coiling in the starting blocks alongside Jesse Owens. It's how we envision Jim Brown rumbling through the Pittsburgh Steelers' famed Steel Curtain defense, anchored by Mean Joe Green.

The combinations are as broad as our imaginations can fathom and limited only by the existence of those athletes who so dazzled us as to make us wonder: What if . . .?

Magic Johnson is among this group, a performer whose game extends so far beyond that of most of his peers that his efforts on the basketball court always stir the imagination.

What if Magic could've played against the Big O?
How 'bout Jerry West?
Man, Magic could've guarded Bill Russell if he wanted to, and then run circles around him on the other end!
Yeah, and Wilt, too!
Can you imagine Magic and Hondo Havlicek goin' at each other?
Or maybe Magic throwin' alley-oop passes to Elgin Baylor? All night, baby, all night!

It's so easy to place Magic Johnson among the most revered talents of any era on any hardwood stage. Close your eyes and he's weaving around and through the defense on any court anywhere, anytime, his 6'-9" frame moving, rolling smoothly through the bodies in his path, his head up, eyes searching. Then he's guarding a young K. C. Jones, staying low against the shorter, more muscular Celtics guard. Later he's threading a blind bounce pass through two defenders and into the hands of Gail Goodrich, who finishes the Lakers' fast-break with an easy lay-up. They make eye contact, an unspoken thanks between teammates. He's hitching up his shorts, bending his knees, and staring down at Oscar Robertson. The Big O is backing, backing, backing into shooting range, then pulling up and aiming for the rim, only to have Magic flick the ball from his grasp as he begins his ascent. Finally, he's staring down the barrel of a gun named Larry Bird beneath the breeze of thirteen championship banners hanging high in the rafters above Boston Garden's famed parquet floor; or he's slamming Isiah Thomas, one of his closest friends in the world, to the ground as the Lakers fight for another title.

All these dreams are possible because when it comes to players like Magic Johnson, those against whom others are judged, the game itself never changes. It's the same in their time as in eras long since entered into the memory banks and history books. Today's players are quicker, certainly. And no doubt bigger, stronger, and more muscular than ever before. Yet the essence of basketball, the game, remains essentially the same, the keys to which are a secret only the legendary players seem to share.

It was no wonder then that in the spring of 1980—Was it really nearly a decade ago?—a wide-eyed-twenty-year-old-still-wet-behind-the-ears-would-be-college-junior point guard stepped toward center court inside the Spectrum in Philadelphia at the onset of game six of the NBA finals and proceeded to create an unfathomable work of art. By the end of the afternoon, Magic Johnson had climaxed his first season as a professional basketball player with a performance for the ages, one widely recognized as the moment when the young player legitimized his apparent quest for greatness. Magic scored 42 points, snatched down 15 rebounds, and passed for 7 assists in a dramatic 123–107 triumph over Julius Erving and the Philadelphia 76ers that clinched the world championship for the Los Angeles Lakers, their first league title in eight years. Yet Magic's exhibition was less remarkable for its statistical brilliance than for another unprecedented aspect of the effort. Not only had Magic helped the Lakers clinch the championship without Kareem Abdul-Jabbar, their legendary center, in California nursing an injured ankle—resting, presumably, for a game seven series finale—but also in one monumental contest he had atoned for the absence of the team's most potent weapon by playing every position on the floor:

center, power forward, scoring forward, shooting guard, and, naturally, point guard.

At tip-off, Magic jumped center against Darryl Dawkins, the 76ers' muscular 6'–11'' 260-pound center. He then skated along the baseline and kissed the ball off the glass and through the net with a gliding, twisting balletic number that seemed to stun Dawkins, his teammates, and the entire sellout crowd. Later, Johnson worked his magic against Bobby Jones, the 76ers' all-defense power forward. He even harassed the legendary Doctor J, the 76ers' explosive, acrobatic scoring forward. Magic also manned both backcourt positions, the so-called scoring guard position, as well as his more familiar role as the Lakers' point guard, the maestro. Wherever he was needed, that's where Magic Johnson was. All told, it was such a commanding performance that it completely overshadowed the effort of one of Magic's teammates, Jamaal Wilkes, who enjoyed the finest afternoon of his career. The player known as "Silk" because of his smooth playing style scored 37 points, complemented by 10 rebounds and 2 assists. But compared to the feats of the Lakers' magical rookie floor leader, Wilkes's accomplishments were relegated to miniscule type in the next morning's daily papers around the country.

That was just a year after Magic had inspired an unheralded Michigan State team that struggled against competition in its own conference, the Big Ten, to the national championship of college basketball with a victory over Indiana State (the team's star was some kid named Bird) in the title game of the annual NCAA tournament. To this day, that contest inside the Salt Palace in Salt Lake City is widely recognized as the most significant in basketball history. The impact it had on the eventual popularity of basketball at the collegiate and professional levels is almost immeasurable. When basketball historians define the birth of the game, they speak of Dr. James Naismith, but when they talk of when the game came of age, they speak of that afternoon in Utah and of two players, Magic Johnson and Larry Bird.

Two years before that contest, Magic led Everett High School in Lansing, Michigan, to the state championship. Thus, within the span of four memorable years, he guided teams to championships on three different levels. On the night of the Lakers' victory over Philadelphia, inside a hotel ballroom where the team celebrated, former NBA star Rick Barry stared toward Johnson for a few seconds, then turned away and shook his head with amazement and fascination. "He thinks every season ends this way," Barry said. "You go to training camp, play a few games, go to the play-offs, then you win a championship. It's unbelievable. Absolutely unbelievable."

In the years since that fairytale beginning in the NBA, Magic has performed as if every season was ordained as the Lakers' championship season. There were pitfalls along the way, certainly, the most dramatic of which was the Lakers' seven-game loss to the Celtics in the 1984 NBA finals, a setback for which Johnson was largely blamed because of the role he played in two of the defeats. After winning the opening game of the series at Boston Garden, the Lakers came within one pass from James Worthy to Johnson of taking a 2–0 lead back home to Los Angeles. But they had to settle for a 1–1 split after Worthy's lackadaisical inbound pass in the final seconds of regulation was picked off by Celtics guard Gerald Henderson, who scored the game-tying basket that sent the contest into overtime where Boston emerged with a victory. (Johnson has since admitted that he should have come toward the ball, but that he didn't see Henderson coming.) Then after taking a 2–1 lead at home in the Forum, the Lakers collapsed when the Celtics began manhandling them in game four. Boston used shock therapy to humble the docile Lakers into submission in an overtime victory that was again marked by a mistake by Magic in the waning seconds of regulation. This time, with the contest tied, he dribbled away an opportunity to win by allowing precious seconds to elapse before trying to float a lazy pass to James Worthy in the low post. It was stolen by Celtics center Robert Parish as time expired, and the Lakers would eventually lose in overtime. Suddenly, a series that might have been a 4–0 sweep was tied 2–2. Thus, sensing that they had dodged a bullet, the Celtics won each of the remaining games on their home court, including the climactic seventh game. Magic still recalls those moments as the lowest of his career. In fact, they haunted him and his teammates for a full year, until the Lakers purged themselves with an emotional payback triumph over the Celtics in the 1985 NBA finals in which the series' clincher was captured inside Boston Garden, where the ghosts of Celtics history had always haunted the Lakers. Never in the history of the franchise (they were once the Minneapolis Lakers) had the Lakers beaten the Celtics in the championship series, so squashing Boston four games to two, with the climactic finale coming on the hallowed parquet floor, was Magic's sweetest moment ever.

Under Magic's growing guidance, the Lakers all but owned the coveted NBA championship trophy during the 1980s, even in the midst of an evolution that would have tripped a team under the guidance of any less a leader. Since his heralded arrival as the number one selection overall in the 1979 collegiate draft, no fewer than three dozen players have donned a Lakers uniform as team management, one of the most respected in the league, sought to read the league's shifting winds each season and create a team that would always contend for the title. To Magic, the most important among his many teammates was Kareem Abdul-Jabbar, the all-time leading scorer in pro basketball history and the player around whom the Lakers were forged in the years after 1975 when he was acquired in the blockbuster trade with the Milwaukee Bucks—one of the most important trades in league history. Eleven years later, the torch was officially passed from Abdul-Jabbar to Magic. That season, Johnson became the team's undisputed conscience and its guiding spirit. By displaying offensive skills that laid dormant during his first seven seasons while maintaining high standards in other areas of his game, Johnson proved himself to be an all-around player on par with Bird, the brilliant Celtics forward who was voted the league's MVP for three successive seasons. Bird's string of trophies ended in 1986–87 when Johnson was named MVP after averaging 23.9 points per game, the most prolific scoring effort of his career. He also grabbed 504 rebounds and led the league with 977 assists. Two seasons later—with Bird missing all but six games because of injuries in both ankles that required surgery and threatened his career—Magic edged out Michael Jordan to win his second MVP award after a season that surpassed even his own standards: 22.5 points, the most of his career; .509 field-goal percentage; 607 rebounds; and 988 assists. He also led the league in free throw shooting for the first time in his career by converting a commanding 91 percent of his shots from the line. Now, from near or far, he was truly Magic.

In between MVP awards, Magic inspired the Lakers to the first of two successive titles by burying the Celtics four games to two in the 1987 championship series. The following season, the Lakers became the first team in nineteen years to successfully defend its crown with a dramatic 4–3 triumph over the emerging Pistons. Last spring, however, Detroit gained the sweetest revenge imaginable, thrusting the defending champions into oblivion with a convincing sweep that served to remind the Lakers that success can be fleeting, erased in a flash. After roaring through the first three rounds without losing a game against Portland, Seattle, and Phoenix, the Lakers endured an unexpected bolt of bad luck. On the eve of the finals, Byron Scott suffered a torn hamstring during a practice drill that would sideline him for the remainder of the play-offs. Then, in the midst of game two at the Palace of Auburn Hills, home of the Pistons, Magic was felled by a torn left hamstring, the same injury that sidelined him for three weeks earlier in the season. He tried to return, starting in game three at the Forum just three days later, hopeful that the adrenaline of playing in front of the hometown crowd would prove to be a curing salve. But after limping about the court for four minutes, Magic knew he was through. Finished—for the series.

Without their starting backcourt, the Lakers were flogged by the Pistons' guards: Isiah Thomas, reserve Vinnie Johnson, and, in particular, the unassuming Joe Dumars, who was eventually named MVP of the championship series.

Once again, Magic had been the focus of the Lakers' fortunes. Or, in this case, their misfortunes. And yet, just as he had done throughout the successes that surrounded his career, he had somehow managed to remain Earvin, to retain the perspective of the young child whose father never allowed him to grow too tall to take out the garbage, rake leaves, and shovel snow. In the hours following Lakers games at the Forum, he's invariably the final player dressed and out of the locker room because of all the well-wishers, autograph seekers, and general admirers who gather around his locker. As each person approaches, Magic offers a smile and a remark, poses for a picture, or gladly scripts his name across a piece of paper.

On the court, Magic Johnson is a one-man clinic on fundamental basketball. To study his performance is to view the essence of the sport, the secrets of basketball brilliance. Of course, there are dynamic moments, last-second shots from improbable distances, forays through defenses that defy mortal logic, and exhibitions of defensive strategy that seem to imply that Magic enjoys some personal insight into the opponents' minds. But for the most part, Magic's game is simple, fundamental basketball. It's reading defenses, predicting an opening before the opposition even realizes it's there. It's rotating from the weak side of the defense in perfect synchronization with his teammates so that one lapse can be converted into points. Most of all, it's winning, winning, and winning again. And it's for everyone, anyone who wishes to watch, enjoy, appreciate, or, yes, even play the game. While so many other players struggle with even the most elementary maneuvers and strategies of the sport, Earvin (Magic) Johnson is one of the few who make basketball brilliance seem so simple, so achievable.

That's Magic's Touch.

Magic's Touch

Whenever the Lakers and Celtics share the same court, it's as if we're playing the last game that will ever be played.

Your Game

Two of my best friends in the world, Isiah
Thomas and Mark Aguirre, won their first championships at my
expense last season. After all of the stretching, the extra conditioning during the off-season, and the rehabilitation I went
through when I first hurt my hamstring in February, I just didn't
want to believe I had become hurt again. I didn't want to
accept it. I was happy—as a friend—for Isiah and Mark, who
have both experienced a lot of frustrating seasons during their
careers. But my joy for them didn't ease my disappointment. The
Pistons are the champions now. But I know how Larry Bird
felt this year. And now I know how we'll both feel next season:
hungry.

Sitting on the sidelines last spring at The Forum near Los
Angeles, in sweat pants and a Lakers T-shirt, that was one of the
hardest things I've ever had to do since I started playing basketball as a kid. Especially because I thought things could have been
different. If I had been able to play, if Byron Scott had been able
to play, I think the Lakers could have won the NBA title for the
third straight year, something that hadn't been done in twenty-
three years, not since the Boston Celtics, our biggest rivals, beat
the Lakers in 1966. Instead, we were both on the bench with
hamstring injuries as the Detroit Pistons swept us in four games
in the NBA finals. The Pistons clinched the series on our home
court and celebrated just around the corner from the Lakers
locker room. The disappointment I felt as I watched them

---

congratulate each other in the final moments, then listened to them through the walls of the Forum, was real and deep. My teammates had played their hearts out, and we had stayed close in every game. But it's not easy for any team to survive injuries. And for me, losing has never been easy to accept. At those moments, I thought about Larry, sitting out almost the entire season with foot injuries as the Celtics struggled through their worst season since Larry joined the team ten years ago.

The Lakers want the title back next year. I'm sure the Celtics will want their shot, too, even though several other teams such as Phoenix, Chicago, New York, Seattle, Houston, Atlanta, and Golden State will have something to say about that. But for me, nothing could be better than the Lakers and Celtics battling it out in the finals one more time.

It doesn't matter whether we're playing inside Boston Garden, with all those championship banners swinging from the sky, that rickety old parquet floor with all its dead spots, the loudest, most dedicated fans in the league, and all those leprechaun ghosts sitting on the opponent's backboard; or if we're at the Forum with the stretch limousines and all the Hollywood stars—Jack Nicholson, O. J. Simpson, Dyan Cannon, Billy Crystal, Arsenio Hall, the Jacksons—sitting at courtside. We can have Dancing Barry rolling out of the stands and the best cheerleaders in basketball, the Laker Girls, making the whole joint crazy during every time-out, or we could be on a playground in the middle of nowhere. Whenever we play the Celtics, it seems like we're playing in the last game that'll be played in basketball history.

And it doesn't matter that the Celtics had to scratch and claw to win the last play-off berth in the Eastern Division in 1989. Whenever Boston's in town, I start feelin' the excitement early that morning when I first wake up, then when I turn on the radio and it's the only thing anybody's talking about. The Lakers and the Celtics are sold-out. Then if I'm home, I feel it again when I come into the locker room a few hours before any game. On most nights everybody's laughin', talkin', and jokin' around, but when the Celtics are waiting for us, it's quiet. The city's buzzin', but we've got to concentrate on what we've got to do.

If we're in Boston, I just try to stay in my hotel room most of the day and shut out the distractions outside. There've been nights—usually the night before the game—when someone has sneaked into the hotel and set off the fire alarm just so we'd lose sleep. After a while, we just expect it to happen. Fans hang out in the lobby in every city, but by the time we're ready to leave for the arena, the lobby in Boston is usually packed. We even have a few supporters in Boston. I don't think they let them buy tickets to the games because by opening tip-off it seems like everybody in Massachusetts is rooting against us.

Last season there were plenty of contenders for the NBA championship. Most people had their eyes on Detroit at the start of the season, but some people picked the Phoenix Suns, whom we eliminated in the conference finals in four games. Some said Atlanta, Chicago, Utah, Seattle, or Cleveland. Overall, it was a strange play-off season because not only were there so many teams with the talent and the experience to come within arms' reach of the title but also nobody picked Boston. They were nowhere to be found.

It had been a crazy year for Boston, no doubt one of the toughest seasons in the entire history of their franchise. Even before Bird decided to sit it out, they were going to have problems because most of their best players, guys like Dennis Johnson, Robert Parish, and Kevin McHale, were all nearing the end of their careers and there weren't a lot of young guys ready to step in and take their places. But then Bird's ankle injury really sent the team into a tailspin.

The last couple of years Chicago and Detroit have come on strong with Michael Jordan and Isiah, but when people talk about the Lakers they still talk about the Celtics, and they always mention me and Bird. It's been that way since our teams played against each other for the NCAA championship in 1979. That game was played in Salt Lake City, and everybody was talking about this guy from Indiana State named Bird. I'd seen him play on television but never in person, and I'd never played against him, so that night it was all I could do to keep from watching him as everybody else was.

Indiana State was undefeated in 33 games going into the championship game, and it was all because of Larry. He was definitely one of the best players I'd ever seen. He could shoot, pass, rebound—he did everything for them. And he was smart. He never made a bad pass or ran a bad play.

We came into the game on a roll, too, although we had struggled a bit during the season and lost some close games, especially in the Big Ten conference where three teams tied for first place, so it was probably more of a surprise that we were in the championship than that Indiana State was there. Bird kept Indiana State in the game almost the whole way, even though we were playing our best basketball of the season. He was shooting the lights out no matter how many guys we had on him, and our strategy was to chase him all over the court, make him pass, make someone else beat us. No matter what we did, he didn't get rattled. He'd pass the ball and hit open guys that we'd almost forgotten about. Our coach, Jud Heathcote, said we defended Bird with "an adjustment and a prayer." He came into the game averaging more than 30 points for his three-year career, but we held him to 19 points, and, miraculously, only two assists. But what impressed me most about Larry came near the end when we were celebrating. He had his head in a towel, crying.

Losing really hurt him, and that's the sign of a true competitor. One of their players went to every guy on his team's bench and told them not to hang their heads because they had played like champions. That guy was right.

Larry and I have played against each other 34 times in the NBA—the Lakers lead our series 20–14—and every time it's like a national event. Reporters from all over the country cover the game, television crews come out of the woodwork, and people start asking us about the game weeks in advance. Our teams faced each other three times in the NBA finals. The Celtics beat us four games to three in 1984. I blew two games in that series in the final seconds because, at that stage of my career, I wasn't mentally ready to handle the responsibility.

We waited a full year to erase those bad memories, and we did the next year when we beat the Celtics in six games. We clinched it on their parquet floor in Boston, which made the victory so sweet I can still taste it. I think that series brought Larry and me closer together. Before that we really didn't know each other. We just kept an eye on each other from across the country. Because we were usually fighting Boston for the best record in the league, every morning I'd check the papers to see how they did. Then I'd sneak a peek at Larry's stats. I missed doing that last year when he was out for all but six games. I only saw him once, when we played the Celtics in Boston. After that game, he came into the Lakers' locker room, long after all the other players were gone, and we talked. We joked around, talked about old times like two guys who'd been retired for twenty years. He said he missed playing and that rehabilitation was boring. He also said he just hoped he could play again.

We've always respected each other, but after that 1985 series, I think the Lakers and Celtics had more respect for each other as teams and I think Larry and I became closer as friends. It would be really nice to see those guys one more time before Larry and I retire. Really nice.

Now almost everywhere I go, whether I'm traveling to another NBA city or walking through the shopping mall, people want to talk basketball. They want to talk about the play-offs, the Celtics, the Pistons, the Lakers, anything. But most of all, they want to talk about the game. They want to know how NBA players play the way we do, how we reached this level.

For myself, I know I was very fortunate to have been coached at an early age by the best teacher in the world—my father. He's the reason I'm playing the way I am now.

When I received my second MVP Award last spring, I thought of him, just as I did in 1987 when I won the award for the first time. He and my mom, who taught me the value of maintaining a down-to-earth perspective on my life, were definitely Most Valuable Parents.

I was still in elementary school in Lansing, Michigan, when dad started taking me out to our driveway and showing me how to play, how to shoot lay-ups with either hand, dribble with either hand, and pass the ball with either hand. I could barely get the ball to the rim, but I loved the game. I was hooked.

Being one of ten kids, it was hard to find ways to be by myself. But I found that with basketball I didn't need anyone else to have a good time, and when I was playing I was having the best time in the world. I think my father sensed this early because he was always willing to spend what little free time he had with me talking basketball. He was a long-time fan, but more knowledgeable than most other guys. So before he'd take me out to the driveway, he'd sit down with me and we'd watch the NBA games on television. Dad made me see the importance of the little things in basketball, the fundamentals, even to players in the pros. Because we lived in Michigan, we got the regional telecasts of the Detroit Pistons' games. Now that I'm playing for the Lakers and the Pistons are one of our biggest rivals, it seems strange that I was once a die-hard Pistons fan. Dave Bing was always my favorite player, so it was weird having him sitting in

My greatest reward is sharing my success with my father.

the stands and rooting against me when we played the Pistons in the finals in the last two seasons. I was only eight years old when he was the first pick in the NBA draft out of Syracuse, but I watched him average 20.0 points a game as a rookie in 1966–67. The next season he led the league in scoring with 27.4 points a game. More important, he helped make the Pistons a competitive team; he tried to help them win. That same year, Detroit reached the play-offs for the first time in franchise history. Pretty soon, on the playground near my house, Main Street Park, everybody was trying to shoot the Dave Bing Jumper, including me. Except, I couldn't jump!

Watching Dave Bing and his teammates with my father was how I learned the simple secrets of basketball. Dad pointed out everything down to the smallest detail—the footwork, the head fakes, the defensive stances, blocking out underneath the boards, things that separated the great players from the good players. Take the Dave Bing Jumper, for instance. Everybody talked about how smooth and cool it was, but the most important thing was that he took the same shot every time. His feet and shoulders were square to the basket, his elbow was at the perfect right angle, he concentrated on the rim, and he followed through. Simple stuff. The basics. After those early film sessions, my father took me out to the driveway and helped me practice what we had seen.

All those sessions began to pay off sooner than I expected. When I got to the seventh grade and went to the gym for basketball tryouts the coach said, "OK, everybody who's right-handed line up on the left side. Everybody who's left-handed line up on the right side. Now shoot lay-ups." Well, anybody who couldn't shoot lay-ups with the opposite hand was cut! The first day! He made no bones about it. As soon as guys went for the shot and couldn't make it, the coach just said, "Cut." I told myself, "Wow, now I know what my dad was saying." So it went from 200 kids to only about 25 just that fast. I was stunned. That day opened my eyes and made me run home and thank my dad.

My father made me understand that playing basketball the way I wanted to play was more than just watching NBA players on television and trying to copy them without any thought, preparation, practice, or any concept about the fundamentals. How could I pass the ball to the open man without learning to see the whole floor and not just one area of it? How could I rebound without learning to block out? How could I score without using my left hand? So I learned the basics first, right from the start. That's when I was on my way toward being in control any time I was on the floor. With the basics, I knew I could counter any move or break down any defender. I also thought I could copy my favorite NBA player. But I soon found out that I was shooting the Dave Bing Jumper when I couldn't jump! That's when I learned that there are some things you just can't control.

My dad also taught me never to be satisfied with developing just one aspect of my game. He said I had to learn to do *everything* at least well. Not perfect, but well enough to be able to rely on any skill whenever I needed it. I had to be able to shoot so that I'd have confidence taking the big shot at the end of the game. I had to learn to block out and rebound so that I could help my teammates on the boards. I had to be able to play defense so I could stop my man down the stretch. I had to be able to dribble with both hands and my head up so that I could get around the pressure defenses. I had to be able to make every kind of pass imaginable so I could get the ball to an open team-mate in any situation. But most important, I had to understand the concepts of the game so that I could make the right deci-sions. I had to learn all of that before I could come inside from that driveway. There's nothing wrong with finding one aspect of the game and staking your reputation on it. That's how a lot of players made it to the NBA. They're known as just great shooters, great passers, great rebounders, or great defenders. But that's all they're recognized for, that one part of their game. But to be known as an all-around player, I knew I had to be at least fun-damentally sound in every part of the game. Not perfect, just sound. It didn't make sense to work so hard on one part of the game I could already do well, like rebounding, then forget about working on my weaknesses. Dad said my opponents would always find my weaknesses, and that it wouldn't take long, at any level, for them to start exploiting me. He said my weaknesses would stand out like a neon sign every time I stepped on a basketball court. If I couldn't dribble with my left hand or if I had a habit of being lazy on defense, everybody would know it right from the beginning. He told me that in basketball I couldn't hide.

Dad helped me keep that perspective by the way he treated me at home. When I got home from games, I still had to take out the trash, no matter whether we won or lost. I still had to rake the leaves, shovel the snow off the driveway, and do my other jobs. By the time I reached high school and started to get some notoriety, Dad always made sure to say, "You're still just Junior, or Earvin, to us." I heard that same tune from all my coaches—George Fox at East Lansing High School, Jud Heathcote at Michigan State, and Pat Riley with the Lakers. None of them treated me any differently than the other players, and I didn't want to be treated any differently, either. I just wanted to be Earvin or Buck, my nickname with the Lakers.

See, I was never caught up in being a "superstar" because, for me, basketball is all about winning. It has never mattered to me who got the job done as long as it got done, even if it's not me. That kind of thinking always helped me keep my perspective, but who am I kidding? It's hard to lose your perspective when you're still taking out the trash.

Every summer for the last few years, I've operated several basketball camps in Detroit, Los Angeles, and San Diego. I get kids from nine years old through seventeen, and, because so many of them have been coming back over and over again, I've seen a lot grow up and become better basketball players. Some kids have come five, six, seven years in a row. One of my former students is a high school varsity coach now, one of the youngest in the country. Some of the guys are in college playing for different teams. Now I'm starting to see a lot of little brothers and sisters of former campers. Pretty soon I'll start seeing sons and daughters, too!

One of the campers I've had is Kareem's son, Kareem, Jr., and his development has really been amazing. He wasn't very good when he first arrived. He was also really shy. Everybody knew he was Kareem's son, which kind of bothered him and made him feel as if everybody expected him to be as good as his father. He'd miss a shot, and kids would yell, "Where's that skyhook?" Kids can be very cruel.

By the second summer Kareem was a much better player, but he was still very quiet. He didn't associate much with the other campers and never took it upon himself to be a leader. Then everything changed by his third summer at the camp. All of a sudden, Kareem, Jr., was a leader. All the kids were following him around and listening to what he had to say. I know the change was just part of his growing up, but I'd like to think the camps and the kinds of things I try to teach the kids helped

"How many times do I have to tell you?
Basketball is hard work!"

bring that side out of him. That's the reward that I get out of the camps, to see kids change and grow, as well as the joy of teaching basketball.

Hosting the camps taught me a lot about working with young people, which has taught me to be patient every time I walk out on a basketball court. There have been many times with the Lakers when I've been frustrated with teammates. Some of them wouldn't work hard. They'd let any little injury keep them out of practice. Or they'd complain about playing time, not shooting the ball enough or anything to get attention. Even as one of the team leaders, I can't always speak right up when I have something to say. I've learned the importance of timing in figuring out how to keep small problems from becoming big ones down the line. Working with the kids also taught me a lot about patience, about understanding what makes people tick, what makes them blend into a team instead of a group of individuals. When the campers first arrive, they usually come in with the idea of just having a good time with Magic Johnson. They think it's gonna be all fast breaks and scrimmages, fancy passes and high-fives, while I put on a one-man show. Boy, are they wrong! I tell them from day one—their parents, too—that if they're being dropped off for a vacation or just a good time then they should load themselves right into the station wagon and go back home. I tell them, "Don't waste your time here because it's gonna be all work. We're going to have a good time, but we'll be working, too. We'll be in the gym early and we'll stay late. You're gonna be tired, hungry, and you might even miss your mom, but if you want to learn to play basketball, this is the place to be." Some of them get scared, but nobody leaves.

Having that kind of attitude is important because, to me, there's only one way to think about this game and one way to play it. That's all out, foot to the floor, pushing myself as hard as I can for as long as I can. I love playing basketball, but one thing is clear. When the ball goes through the net, the *team* gets two points. A player hardly ever scores by himself. To make any basket happen, somebody played good defense, somebody boxed out, somebody got the rebound, somebody hustled down the floor, somebody set the pick, somebody got open, somebody passed the ball, and somebody hit the shot. That's a lot of somebodies, but a lot of somebodies equals a team. Basketball is a team game where no one player is more important than the team. I might score all the points in the world, but if the other team won by 1 point, I don't have anything to be happy about. On Christmas Day 1984, I watched Bernard King score 60 points against the New Jersey Nets on national television. But afterward he wasn't celebrating or even bragging. "What does it matter?" he said, "We lost." That's my kind of guy. Playing basketball is about trying to win for the *team* and not yourself.

I always tell my campers that goes double for those of them who are the "stars" on their teams back home. On the Lakers, we believe we're all stars, from the starters to the last man on the bench. Everybody plays a role in the team's success. When they hand out championship rings, they don't just give them to the MVP. Everybody gets one. Twelve guys, twelve rings. *The team*.

I've also learned in my camps that I can't be tough all the time. Sometimes, I've got to be soft and understanding. For some of the younger kids, the camp is their first time away from home for a long period of time, so I don't want to scare them so much that they never want to leave home again. I try to be outgoing and open, too, as well as stern. It can lead to some funny times. One day between sessions, I was coming around a corner where there were a few of the kids on the other side. They couldn't see me, but I could hear them. As I've said, I'm hard on them. I drive them because I believe in working hard. It worked for me, so I'm convinced that's how you become a better player. Hard work is the basis of everything you do on the basketball court. Almost any NBA player will tell you that. Hard work and concentration. But I'm fair, too; at least *I* think I am.

This day as I was coming around the corner, I heard one of the kids say, "That Magic Johnson, he's so mean! I thought he was nice. He hasn't smiled since he's been here." So here I come to the top of the stairs. I sneak up behind them and yell, "What are you doin'?! Why aren't you in the gym?!" They all started stammerin', stumblin', and runnin' for shelter. So I said, "So you don't think I smile, huh? Well, here's a smile. Now, get back in the gym!" I laughed when they left, then I thought to myself, "Man, am I *that* hard on them?" The saddest thing about the camps comes at the end of each session when the kids have to leave. Some of them jump into my arms and say, "I don't want to go!" or "Can I have another week?" A lot come back, or they write and tell me how well they're doing back home. That makes me feel good, even though I'm so "mean."

"If you guys are going to play defense against Larry Bird, you're going to have to do better than that."

Most of the kids who come to the camps are surprised about the amount of hard work I ask them to do. That's because it's hard for most people to know the hard work needed to play the game really well when they just watch NBA players on television. Most of the players in the league are so good they make the game look easy, as if it's so natural. The average fan doesn't understand what the players have to go through, the hours of practices and dedication, to make it look that easy. They don't believe Larry Bird took 1000 jump shots in a gym all by himself before almost every game. They don't believe Mark Eaton of Utah studies films of opposing players for hours so he can understand their shooting habits and become a better shot-blocker. And they don't believe Michael Jordan works on his moves over and over and over again before going out and embarrassing some poor defender. That's because everything that happens on the floor happens so fast that, unless you've studied the game or played it, you can't always see *why* certain things happen or you can't really understand how difficult a particular move was, even one that looked so easy. But the guys at the top of the game, the players who make the all-star teams every year, have all perfected the fundamentals, the little unnoticeable skills that usually play a role in determining the outcome of the game. Those players have learned the fundamentals so well you hardly notice them. They pump fake, follow through, complete the bounce pass, and box out so fast that it's usually overlooked. For instance, I used to hear all the time that Larry Bird and I can't jump. Well, we get by, and the reason is sound fundamentals and hard work. That's why in my camps I make sure the campers run the drills over and over again, so many times it makes them dizzy. But it's worth it. Most of them can't complete the drills the first time around, but sooner or later it just clicks. *Bam!* They'll say, "Wow, that's easy." That's when I smile.

Still through all of my years of running camps, I've never tried to change a kid's game, his natural playing style. And I'm smart enough to know my advice won't turn every camper into another Michael Jordan, Larry Bird, or Kareem Abdul-Jabbar. All I want to do in my camps and with this book is to give young players a chance to see how good they can be, how far they can go in this game. It's wrong to try to change someone into something they're not. Everybody has their own style, something players call "your game." It's not someone else's; it's your's. There's nothing wrong with trying to mimic the way a friend or an idol plays, just as I did in trying to be another Dave Bing. But I never let my childhood dreams take away from what I did best and how I could best help my team win. Some people have an almost natural way of dribbling and shooting, so trying to change their style rather than simply helping them with the fundamentals—and there's a difference—only makes players uncomfortable, which hurts their game. Two classic examples that come to my mind are Jamaal Wilkes, who was once one of my teammates, and Michael Adams, the Denver Nuggets' point guard. Jamaal always had a funny motion with his shot, sort of twisting it around his head rather than coming straight over the top. Sometimes I didn't know how he ever got it off without getting it blocked. But he did, to the tune of 14,644 points during twelve seasons in the NBA. Michael Adams shoots like a shot-putter might play basketball. He's only 5'-8", so he must have had to shoot like that when he was younger, smaller, and probably not strong enough to get the ball all the way to the rim by shooting it with a regular motion. Well, Jamaal became an all-star who made about half his shots during his career, while Michael is one of the league's deadliest 3-point shooters. Not bad for a couple of guys who shoot funny. Obviously, they were smart enough to resist the people who tried to change their styles. Instead, they just continued to study the game, improve their skills, and become smarter players, students of the game. At my camps, I try to give the campers the tools that'll make it easier for them to accomplish their goals. I want them to be able to take what they do best on the basketball court and do it better. However they shoot or however they dribble, maybe one small adjustment can make all the difference in the world to their game. I see so many kids who make bad passes because they're trying to make the fanciest pass before they've learned the proper way to make the easy pass. I see kids shooting jumpers from beyond the 3-point circle before they've learned to make a lay-up with both hands or learned how to shoot with the proper form. That's wrong.

Even in the NBA, it's surprising how many players have trouble shooting lay-ups and free throws, even though they're two of the easiest shots in the game. I want my campers to learn the proper blocking-out techniques and to develop the right attitude about rebounding before they just start jumping after every rebound. Watching guys like Buck Williams, Moses Malone, and Akeem Olajuwon will make anyone realize that there's more to rebounding than just jumping. And I want them to learn how to play good, solid, hard-nosed defense before trying to make steals or block shots. And I want them to be in condition because a tired player will always look for the easy way out, make defensive mistakes, or probably lose concentration. To me, there is no easy way to play basketball. Not one.

I didn't always understand that. When I was in high school, I sometimes took basketball for granted. Like most kids my age, when things were going well I tried to see what I could get away with from the coach. Sometimes, the coach would protect you, maybe let you go without being punished. But this time I was testing Coach Fox. I was also letting my ego overtake my common sense. Well, the coach put my ego back into place by telling me something I'll never forget. He was the type of coach who made everyone on the team feel as if he was an equal part of the team. It didn't matter whether you were a starter or a bench player, you did everything the team did. You ran laps, you did the drills, and you worked hard during practice, every practice. That's why the environment was such a comfortable one for all the players and probably why we won so many games. He was loose but firm. His one rule was that everybody had to work hard, no excuses. This particular day, I was just playing around in practice. I didn't feel like being there, so I didn't take the drills seriously. I ran everything at half-speed and tried to laugh it off. Well, he came to me and whispered in my ear. He said, "Earvin, if you come tomorrow with the same attitude and practice the same way, you won't start the next game." That was my wake-up call. It was the one and only time that happened to me, and I never had another problem like that through high school, college, or the pros. What Coach Fox said that day always stayed with me and remained on my mind. From then on, I knew I always had to work hard, no matter whether I was at practice or in a game. What I learned was that performances in games are directly related to performances in practice. If I didn't practice hard, I probably wouldn't play hard or wouldn't have the energy to play hard down the stretch when it's most important.

I stress to the kids at my camp that I haven't stopped working hard. They know I'm at the gym at 5 AM when I don't have to be there until 6 AM. I'm at practice earlier than anybody because that's when I can get things done without any interruptions. I can work on the kinds of skills that fill out my all-around game and make me a better player. That's still my routine every

During my numerous speaking engagements to various youth groups, I stress that hard work and discipline can help make you both a better athlete and a better person.

summer because I still love the game so much. I tell them that the more they love basketball, the earlier they should be at practice. The guys who do that are usually the ones who become the best players. One of the first questions asked at every session is, "How long do we practice?" My answer's always the same: "How long? What do you mean, 'How long?' You go until it's either too dark or you just can't go anymore. Basketball is hourless. You can't just say two hours or three hours. It's just go. You might look up, and three hours will have passed. Then you turn around and say, 'Man, get me some spotlights out here. I want to go some more!' You just go until you have to go home to your parents. You go until the job's done."

Since my lesson from Coach Fox, discipline has been a big factor in my success, and not just on the basketball court. Not having discipline is the biggest problem a lot of kids bring to my camp. If they can learn discipline, then everything else will fall into place, whether it's in basketball or life away from the gym. My dad taught me that if I don't work just a little harder than the other guy, maybe stay a little longer after practice, then my efforts wouldn't pay off. Without hard work, I wouldn't have become what I wanted to be, whether it was an NBA player or a successful businessman. Whatever I wanted out of life, I knew that it was up to me to achieve it.

Kareem taught me a few tricks. I hope I taught him some, too.

2

Seein' Is Believin'

On normal nights at the Forum, you feel the crowd's highs and lows the whole time. But tonight, the Pistons are on tap, and the energy's so high; it's just me and the game.

It's a couple of seconds after tip-off; the place is rocking, but to me the arena's silent, except for the sounds of sneakers, guys bumping, and the two coaches screamin' on the sidelines. I'm dribbling the ball near the top of the circle, just at the 3-point line. Byron Scott, our other guard, is about to run around a double screen by Kareem and A. C. Green, so the defense will probably switch. That'll leave Mark Aguirre guarding Byron in the corner and Isiah down in the low post with A. C., who's 6'-9''. Both of those'll be mismatches unless Isiah can get around that double screen. James Worthy's out on the other side waiting to see what develops. If Byron's covered, he'll cut into the lane and post Rick Mahorn. I like that matchup because James is too quick for Mahorn; so let's see what happens.

OK, here comes Byron. He's flying around the screen, so I'll pass him the ball. Man, Isiah gets over the top and into Byron's face just in time so he couldn't shoot. Here goes James cutting across the lane. Byron gets him the ball instead of trying to force the shot. James tries to spin, but Aguirre's come over and gotten in his face so fast he can't move. Where's A. C.? He's cutting to the basket, just as we went over in practice. Pat told us,

"When they double team, cut and look for the pass." We prepared for this, so James knew right where A. C. would be. Without even looking, he flicked a bounce pass in the lane that hit A. C. in full stride.

But here comes Bill Laimbeer, leaving Kareem to try and block A. C.'s shot. Man, the Pistons are rotating fast tonight! A. C. could try to dish the ball over to Kareem, but he's already in the air. Oh man, A. C.'s gonna try and jam over Laimbeer. Bam! He did it. And he was fouled. All right! A chance for a 3-point play.

I go over and congratulate A. C., but I don't forget James or Byron because they read the defense so well in the first place, then executed the play just like we practiced it, so everything clicked. Nobody forced anything. It was the team that made that play work, so high-fives all around, baby.

Now some people might think that the 24-second clock would've gone off long before all that could have happened. Not really. All that action happened in about 15 seconds, maybe less. When most fans watch an NBA game, whether they're in the stands or at home in front of the television, they probably see a bunch of players running up and down the court, then crisscrossing back and forth before someone takes a shot. Then the players charge the other way and do it all over again. They usually watch the player with the ball. He either passes, shoots, or commits a turnover. Then you see everybody run the other way and watch it happen all over again. Well, maybe a novice would be satisfied with that action, but anyone who really understands the game knows there's much more to playing basketball than that. When a team's working together as one unit, the game is like clockwork—fast and efficient. It's Boom! Bam! Dish! and Jam! Blink and you might miss the key part of the sequence that opened the play for someone to finally score. That's why the game is so difficult to watch for some fans, unless they've done their homework.

I was lucky that my father taught me exactly how to watch a game when I was still young. He taught me how to see everything happening on the floor and not just the action in one corner or even one-half of the floor. He taught me the game by watching films, even when I was in junior high school, and by showing me why plays like the pick-and-roll, backdoor, simple things like that, worked when they were run correctly. He showed me how they developed, what they looked like in the early stages so that I would learn to recognize situations before the other players would. He told me that if I could do that I'd be able to take advantage of the openings before the defense even sees them. He wanted me to see things before they even happened.

Fans always tell me they have trouble trying to watch a basketball game. They see the ball, so they know when someone scores, but they can't catch the quick moves or see the strategies develop until it's too late, such as after a basket's been scored, or when the defense has made the steal, or when a player has had his shot blocked and the other team is already on its way down the floor. Basketball's a simple game to play and watch, but only if you develop an eye for even the smallest details of the game and see it the way players and coaches do, as ten bodies working together and against each other, bumping and pounding, and not just a bunch of guys going one on one.

To get the true flavor of the game, I tell people to try another angle, to focus on the center, the man in the middle. All the action, whether it's on the ball or away from it, revolves around that position. People who watch the center won't miss anything. They'll see the offensive movement, the screens, and picks teams use to get someone an open shot. They'll also see defensive rotations and adjustments. If they watch only the basketball, they'll miss a lot of the game on the other side of the floor, the weak side, things that ultimately might be the reason the team with the ball either scores or doesn't.

For us, everything revolved around Kareem from the moment I arrived for my first training camp in 1979 until the 1986–87 season when Pat Riley restructured our attack and focused most of it around me. But until Kareem retired at the end of the 1988–89 season, he was still our man in the clutch when we really needed to score. We wouldn't have won back-to-back championships by beating the Pistons in 1988 without Kareem because he hit two big free throws in the final seconds of game six after being fouled by Bill Laimbeer. We were down three games to two at the time, so without that victory our season would have been over. As the team's point guard, I almost always had the basketball, but almost everything I read about the defense went through him. The screens, the cuts, the openings, they all keyed on Kareem. He was our anchor during my first ten seasons. I was lucky to have played with him.

"OK, fellas, these guys are in trouble."

To *really* watch a game, you have to think like a player. Sometimes I tell fans to pretend they're the point guard, to look for an opening in the defense, a weakness. They should see if they can catch the defensive player leaning the wrong way before the offensive player drives around him; or if they can see the offensive player read a defensive double team and dish the basketball off to the open man who's cutting to the basket; or if they can see the defensive player creeping toward an open lane because he reads the eyes of the player with the basketball and sees that the spot is where he's about to pass it; or if they can notice the center on defense sliding across the lane to help a teammate who's been beaten by his man, then arriving just in time to block the opponent's drive; or if they can catch it before the players do, so when someone makes the pass they can say, "Yeah, I made that pass, too," or when someone makes a steal they can say, "Yeah, that defensive player saw the same thing I did." Fans can pretend they're Larry Bird staring down at the unlucky guy who's been assigned to guard him, daring him to make a defensive move. When the defender backs off just a little, they shoot the jumper. If he comes up and crowds them, they give him Larry's little head fake then go right around him. Or they can pretend they're Michael Jordan. They put their wings on, then come flying down the floor, stalking the defense, their tongue wagging out of the side of their mouth, looking for somebody to dunk on. Everybody's mesmerized. They see an opening in the lane. They fake right, roll left, take off, and jam it through over two players who didn't have a chance. Then on their way back to the defensive end of the floor, they pass the other team's coach and say, "That guy can't guard me! You'd better get somebody out here who can guard me before that guy gets hurt!"

Watching the game can be so much more fun for fans when they begin to think like the players. The most successful basketball players at any level see the game in their minds. They size up situations, then see plays an instant before they happen. They've learned to look at the court in a way that's different from most other players and fans. Some former players who've gone into coaching get frustrated because most of their players just don't see the game the way they did. Guys like Lenny Wilkens, Willis Reed, Doug Collins were special players because of not only what they could do on the floor but also they had a mind for the game that some of their opponents and teammates didn't. That's not something coaches can just pass on to the players they coach if they simply can't absorb it.

I understand what they go through. Early on, when I first began coaching kids at my summer camps, I got caught up in that same kind of thinking and became frustrated, too. During a scrimmage, I'd stop play and yell at a kid because he didn't see a teammate who was open for an easy shot, or he missed that a particular passing lane was clear, or he wasn't paying attention on defense and his man slipped right by him for an easy lay-up. I had to learn that the kids couldn't see what I saw, that the game I was playing in my mind was a lot different than the game they were playing on the floor. To me, everything was clear. It was like a book where everything was explained down to the smallest detail and illustrated with pictures that were clear and strong. But to a lot of people, the game was too fast and too complicated to see. The pictures were blurry. That's unfortunate because if people would learn to visualize the game, to see it and think it the right way, then everything on the floor becomes crystal clear. It becomes a whole new game.

Running the fast break is my favorite part of the game. No question, this is the most exciting part of basketball, when you're coming down the floor full-speed, looking in front, to the side, and behind you. In those few seconds, players on both sides of the ball are making every decision imaginable. It all starts when the team gets the rebound and everyone does an about face and starts charging to the other end of the floor. When the break starts to develop, spectators will miss all the real action if they just watch the player with the basketball. They'll miss the wingmen break out wide and line themselves up to get the pass from the man with the ball. They'll miss the defensive guys backpeddling and trying to decide who they're going to cover or which way they're going to try to force the play. Just watching the ball, they'll miss all of that, all of those strategies that are really the core of the game, the interaction of the players on both sides of the basketball. A fan should want to see the whole game develop. They should want to see what the players see and begin to think along with them. Why'd Magic decide to pass the basketball to Byron Scott in the corner rather than A. C. Green inside? (Because Byron's man had come over to double team me and he was wide open at his favorite spot on the floor.) Why didn't Magic see Michael Cooper open in the corner? (Yeah, but because of a defensive switch, Mychal Thompson, who is 6'–10", was

My teammate James Worthy finishes a play with a slam dunk—a sure two points— against the Boston Celtics' Larry Bird and Kevin McHale.

being guarded by a 6'–3'' guard in the post. Always take advantage of this kind of mismatch.) Why'd Magic give the ball up to Kareem on the break rather than to James Worthy on the wing? (Because Kareem made a great defensive play at the other end to block a guy's shot, then he hustled down the floor before his man got there. I was rewarding him.) People in the stands who can ask those kinds of questions are the true basketball fans.

If fans can anticipate what's about to happen on the floor, that's what players call having a "feel for the game." If I'm trying to defend a player who has that feel, he knows what I'm going to do even before I do. He knows how I'm going to react to certain plays even before my arms and legs know which way they're going to go. And contrary to what so many people believe, that most of the fanciest plays are done on instinct, players with a feel for the game learn to complete those plays with concentration, practice, and dedication. Younger players may not grow to be 7 feet tall, but neither did Spud Webb or Tyrone (Mugsy) Bogues and they became NBA players because they worked hard to develop the skills that would take them to the highest level of the game. And they studied the game. They learned how to play the game. For the average fan, learning how to watch them play can be just as much fun.

Even basketball fans who've never played the sport can develop a feel for the game from the stands. So more than just knowing the score, they'll know how to read the importance of different scoring margins and how each team is reacting to either being ahead or behind. Good teams are always capable of erasing almost any lead. So they'll watch closely the team that's ahead and look for signs that they're satisfied with the lead. That's the most dangerous thing that can happen to a team, but it happens to almost everybody. In December of 1988, the Lakers blew a 20-point lead against the Washington Bullets at the Capital Centre in Landover, Maryland. That's because we got lazy. We were in the middle of a slump, and we weren't playing well; we were so happy to get a lead, we relaxed. Before we knew it, it was their game again, and with their crowd behind them, we just couldn't regain control. It was embarrassing. That's one game *no one*, except maybe Bullets' fans, should want to see through my eyes.

From the stands, spectators can also become the coach. If a team scores three or four times in a row against the home team, do you call time-out? Do you make a substitution? Do you yell at the players for making mistakes or encourage them to just play harder and concentrate? Do you let the players on the floor ride out the storm? If one particular player is hot, if he's just running his defender in circles, do you call his play again? And again? Or do you use him as a decoy to set up someone else for the shot? If the player misses badly, do you call his play again? Do you rest him? Do you allow the rookie to play through his mistakes, even though it might cost the team some points? Or do you risk shattering his confidence by taking him out? And what about your reserves? Are you concerned that they get at least a few minutes of playing time? Do you reward them for practicing hard or just let them know that the games are only for the starters and two or three other key players? Decisions, decisions.

All these questions are being asked on the floor as the game is being played, which is why basketball is such a fascinating game. The players and coach are trying to answer them every moment we're out on the floor. Those questions should be going through the fans' minds as they're watching any game, no matter whether it's a game between kids, teenagers on the playground, adults at the YMCA or YWCA, or boys and girls on teams in junior high, high school, or college. Think the game as well as play it.

To me, basketball is a labor of love, and I'd like to help anyone who either plays the game or just watches it to enjoy it more, understand it more, or play it better. Besides winning championships, that's my reward. Every time a fan comes up to me and says I helped bring them into basketball, I smile, and that's what this book is all about.

Here I am as a freshman at Michigan State University, eager to lead the Spartans to an NCAA championship.

3

The World on a String

Picture this tall, skinny kid about ten years old dribbling a basketball down the street. Not occasionally but every day; that was me. I'd take my basketball everywhere. If I was going on an errand for my mother, I'd dribble on the sidewalk, making a game out of trying to miss the cracks. Or I'd dribble one block right-handed and one block left-handed. Then I'd dribble home with a sack of groceries in my arm. Wherever I was going, I'd be dribblin' my basketball. The game was just in me. I'd dribble while I was just sittin' on the porch. I'd be so noisy that the neighbors would come out of their houses. They would be so mad at me for making all that noise! When I was going down the street, people looked at me all the time as if I was strange. I can see 'em now. But because I was so young, they just shook their heads and said, "That's Earvin." The only place I wasn't allowed to dribble was in the house. I knew the rules, even though I sometimes broke them. On rainy days, I'd play sock basketball; I'd just roll up two or three pairs of socks and dribble and shoot all day. I'd pretend I was different teams. One day I could be the Pistons beating the Celtics or the Bulls beating the Knicks. I'd win two or three world championships in one night. All the time, my Mom was cool. She knew I was just going for it.

Being so crazy about dribbling was probably the one thing that most helped my game when I was young. By the time I was in the fourth grade, I was playing in four different leagues. Every day, I was somewhere—at the YMCA, the church, or the local recreation center. I even played on Sundays; I couldn't wait to get home from church and get out of my suit—my only suit—and get down to the park to play. You know I dribbled all the way there. After hours and days and months and years of dribbling all over town and every different way—behind my back, between my legs—that basketball was like a part of me, like another arm. By then, I just had the touch, and it was as if the ball wasn't there. That's what dribblin' is—touch. Once I got it, I knew the game was under my control. I wanted to be able to feel the ball without looking at it. I wanted it to go where I went without fighting it or searching for it. I wanted to be able to make all my fanciest moves, spinning and twisting for the basket, and have the ball be right there in my hand. When I was coming down the floor against the defense, I wanted to keep my head up so I could see the whole floor, not looking down to search for the basketball. The only way I could do that was to have the touch.

I was also lucky enough to get to see some of the best dribbling artists of all time do their thing. When I was a kid, my dad took me to see the Harlem Globetrotters and Harlem Magicians every year. It was a real treat. They'd do all the tricks for the crowd. Like everybody else, I laughed when they threw the fake water on the crowd, but when they were really playing, I was watching the basketball. My favorite part was when the guys would make a circle and do tricks to the song "Sweet Georgia Brown." I was always amazed by that part. Everybody else would be laughing and having a good time while I'd be saying to myself, "Man, how'd they do that?" Marques Haynes was my hero when it came to dribbling. I always thought it was a shame that guys like him, those who played on all-black teams like the New York Rens, didn't get to play in the NBA because they happened to come along before the league allowed black players. They could have played with *anybody* in the league. Marques would get down on his knees and start dribbling; then he would get lower and lower until he was lying on the floor, still dribbling the basketball. Nobody could get it away from him, either. The players from the other team might have been there to lose to the Globetrotters, but I knew the one player assigned to Marques was trying to steal the ball. This was one part of the show where they could try as hard as they wanted and it wouldn't make any difference. Marques never looked at the ball; he always kept his eye on the guy trying to take the ball away from him. He was able to keep it away because, every time the defender made a motion one way or the other, Marques would be able to evade him just as quick.

The next day at the playground, everybody was trying to be Marques. You might come down the court, then put it between your legs or behind your back, different things like that. The guys would yell, "Marques Haynes!" or "Globetrotter!" Times like that made dribbling fun, which made all the ballhandling drills and practices fun, too.

The Globetrotters and Magicians had one trick where they replaced the real basketball with a fake one that had a rubber band attached to it. Almost everyone who's seen one of those teams, and that's just about everybody, knows it. The player passed the basketball, but before it got to the other player, it came flying back right into the hands of the guy who made the pass. It was funny! But to me, it also seemed like the ideal control to have with the basketball. Obviously, I couldn't have the ball on a string so that it went everywhere I did, but I thought I could come close. I know some guys say now that I palm the basketball. Carrying it is illegal, but I try to keep it under my control as long as I can without breaking the rules. That's how I can get through two defenders, around two others, and over the fifth before dishing off for the jam. It's the touch.

There are some players in the league I envy because of what they can do with the basketball. Being a fan as well as a player, I sometimes get caught up watching guys like Isiah Thomas, Kevin Johnson, and Mark Jackson doing things I wish I could do. Being 6'-9" limits me because I have to bend my knees and back so much just to stay low. But these guys are all just over 6', so they can go through you even with dozens of hands down there trying to take the ball away. I'll be on the sidelines saying, "No way!" But they can handle it. It's just like my teammate David Rivers in practice. He can really handle the ball, just as if it's on a string. His only problem is that he tries to go through too many guys, tries to do too much. He just needs to learn to look at the defense more. But if you're talking about getting down low and going through the gaps, he can do it. Me, I've got to *push* it through the defense to get through the gaps, whereas the smaller guys can *dribble* it through. I wish I could do that.

When players improve their ball-handling skills, it opens up a whole new basketball world for them, no matter how old they

Teams like Phoenix are trying to block our path to the championship, but we're still driving for the ring.

are or what level they've reached. No one's ever too old to learn another skill. When anyone thinks he's too old to learn, it's time for him to quit. These days, even NBA players have to continue to improve. There are too many good young players coming out of college, and too many guys still trying to break into the league from places like the Continental Basketball Association and Europe. The minute someone gets satisfied with his game, he's usually gone.

One of the obvious areas is ball handling; everything begins with how well a player handles the ball. The more comfortable he becomes, the more he can concentrate on other areas of the game. During every off season, Pat Riley sends each Laker a letter telling him the areas of his game he should work on over the summer. He doesn't demand improvement, but it's a strong suggestion and he's hardly ever off the mark. Each year we won the championship, it was partly because every player followed the coach's suggestions and improved his game. But it shouldn't be up to the coach to suggest improvements. A player's got to take that upon himself. For everything a player can do this season that he couldn't do last season, the team becomes better.

Take A. C. Green, for example, the Lakers' power forward. In his first few seasons, A. C. couldn't dribble around his man at all. Teams knew he wasn't comfortable handling the ball, so when he tried they attacked him immediately. It wasn't a comfortable situation for him or anyone else. Now that's all changed. A. C. can get the rebound and start the fast break himself if he has to, at least for a couple of dribbles. That's a major advantage for a running team like the Lakers because if the rebounder can put the basketball on the floor and get the fast break started, then we probably can beat at least one defender, maybe more. That's all we need, and we're gone.

Another teammate, Byron Scott, who starts alongside me at guard, also has improved his ball handling over the last few years and has helped the team. Early in his career, all Byron could do was shoot the jumper. He was a deadly shooter, but he wasn't comfortable putting the ball on the floor and driving. The defense knew this, so they just played him tight. They refused to give him any room to shoot because they knew he wouldn't try to go around them. Now, Byron can pump fake and go to the hole as well as anybody. That forces defense to play him honestly, and that gives us more options. So there's no question

Against top defenders like Dennis Rodman of Detroit, the league's best defensive player in 1988–89, I have to keep my head up and use my fingertips to control the ball.

that when A. C. Green and Byron Scott became better ball handlers, the Lakers became a better team.

I see three important factors to dribbling. One, as I've mentioned, is that you've got to keep your head up. When I'm coming down the floor on the fast break with Maurice Cheeks in front of me and Charles Barkley trying to catch me from behind, I have to keep my head up or somebody's going to take the ball away from me. And that's a turnover in my book, which is the worst thing you can find in the box score next to your name.

During my career, I've committed almost 2700 turnovers! Nearly 3000 mistakes! And I remember almost every one; they're my nightmares. Most of them came when I didn't look at what I was doing. Either my head wasn't up, or my eyes weren't *really* open to what I was doing. I try to console myself about all those mistakes by remembering that I've also played more than 26,000 minutes. That comes out to almost one turnover for every 10 minutes I play. That's not so bad. But all it takes is one turnover at the wrong time to lose the game.

The second important aspect of dribbling is positioning. I'd love to be able to dribble down so low that I could control and protect the ball better; but because of my height, I'm usually up higher than the guy who's defending me. Still, I get down as low as I can with my dribble, so low I'm almost like Mugsy Bogues or Spud Webb.

When I'm dribbling I want to be a little guy because, when I'm going one on one against a defender, I want to protect the ball by using my other hand as a shield. I can't be too obvious about it, or I'll get called for an offensive foul. But I keep my arm extended just enough so that when my man tries to go for the steal he has to go through me and probably commit a foul. I also want to keep my feet a comfortable width apart while I'm dribbling. I do that to make those quick moves and remain on balance and in control. When I'm in control, I can spin either way or put the ball behind my back or between my legs to elude a defender. I couldn't do any of that if my legs were too close together or too wide apart. I might also trip over myself, and that's the most embarrassing thing that could happen.

I like to keep my feet a shoulders' width apart. For some players, it's wider; for others, a little closer together, but there's not many. Watch the players who don't commit a lot of turnovers, guys like John Stockton, Maurice Cheeks, or Mark Price. Their legs are spread wide, and knees are bent in perfect position.

I protect the ball by using my free arm as a shield.

I love watching my buddy Isiah dribble the basketball. He's so good that he has to hold himself back in games so he doesn't look as though he's trying to make somebody look bad. But every once in awhile, he just can't control himself. Sometimes he comes down the floor on the break with only one defender in front of him. When we're playing the Pistons, I hate to be that guy because I just *know* Isiah's going to do something that'll make me look as though I don't know which way is up.

He comes down the floor, and when he gets to the top of the key he stops. He's still dribblin', and he's just staring at the guy in front of him, daring him to try and stop him. Then all of a sudden, he'll bounce the ball about twenty-five times really quick between his legs. *Rat-tat-tat-tat-tat-tat-tat-tat!* Just like that. It sounds like a machine gun. It usually makes the defender freeze for just a split second, and that's all Isiah needs to go by the guy and make the easy lay-up.

Even on the road when Isiah does that move, the place goes wild. You know how embarrassing it is to have your own crowd going crazy over a move that makes you look bad? When he does it to me, I just shake my head and go on. What else can I do? Except come back and win.

Finally, there's the third element of dribbling. It's the most important because it's actually putting your hand on the basketball. That's not as simple as it sounds. You see some players trying to dribble the ball with their palm. That's wrong! Touch your hand and tell me where the most sensitive areas are. It's the fingertips, right? That's where you've got the most delicate touch. So that's where you want to keep the basketball, on your fingertips, like someone that you'd treat with tender loving care. You can control the ball with your fingers better than your hand. If you don't believe me, try it. Dribbling the ball with the palm of your hand won't create anything but blisters. Using your fingers will make sweet music.

Believe it or not, getting down on the floor and dribbling the ball like Marques Haynes still helps improve my ball-handling skills. I call it the *six-inch drill*. I lie on the court, all the way down on my side until I'm resting my head on my hand and my elbow on the floor. Then I dribble the ball, only about six inches from the floor, with my other hand. This is how you develop control.

The next step to try is the *figure-eight drill*. Stand up and spread your legs wide apart; now begin by dribbling the ball with

All those years of dribbling the ball down the streets of East Lansing are still paying off. Now, I can keep my mind on the game.

your right hand close to the ground. Move the ball through your legs until you can transfer it to your left hand behind your left leg. Slowly dribble the ball around your left leg until it's in front, then go back between your legs until you pick it up with your right hand behind your right leg. This is another control drill.

Dribbling between your legs and behind your back used to be considered "hot-dogging." Now it's not. Sometimes you've got to put the ball between your legs to elude the defender coming from the side. And when you're bringing the ball up the court, most teams will try to make you change directions just to kill some time off the clock. It's easy to do, but if you don't keep your head up and have complete control of the ball, your man will make the steal and you'll be heading for the bench.

The final drill is the *wall drill*. Take the basketball and try to dribble it against the wall, but from only about 2 inches away. It's hard; gravity will pull the ball down. But this will help strengthen your fingers and help you learn to maintain control when someone gets their hand on the ball and tries to force it away. *Please* don't try this drill at home. Use a wall at the park or in the gym, anywhere but at home. Don't get me in trouble.

When I can get my opponent off balance, I'll always find the open man.

Givin' It Up

4

Just about everyone who talks about the way I play basketball talks about my passing first; then they mention my rebounding because I'm so tall for a guard; and *then* they might get around to talking about my scoring. That's how I've made my reputation, as somebody who shares the ball and gets everybody involved. But believe it or not, I used to dominate games as a scorer. I was a regular Michael Jordan scoring machine. Unstoppable.

OK, so I was in elementary school, in third, fourth, and fifth grades playing in the church leagues and recreational leagues that were all over East Lansing. But a Michael Jordan at any age is still a Michael Jordan, right? Well, that was me. They called me "Little Earvin," except back then I wasn't so little compared to the other kids my age. My height was my best weapon. Nobody ever called 3 seconds in those leagues, so I had a party right underneath the basket. I was so tall that I'd just hang out in the lane, rebound the basketball, and take off for the other end of the court. This is where all those years of dribbling back and forth to the grocery store for my mother finally paid off. By then, dribbling was what I did best.

At that age, the kid who was the best dribbler was always the star of the team. Most kids that young can't control the basketball for more than three or four bounces, if that many. And defensively, nobody realizes how to take the ball away from somebody without committing a foul; so once I was gone,

43

somebody on the other team had to foul me to keep me from shooting a lay-up. There I was, Not-so-Little Earvin, dribbling from one end of the floor to the other and shooting the lights out of the gym! If my team scored 26 points, I'd usually have 22. If we scored 15, I'd have 13.

My teammates didn't have any problems with me shooting so much and doing all the scoring because we won almost all of our games. When you win, nobody's mad. It was my teammates' parents who got upset with me. They didn't care who won. They just came to see their kids play, and they wanted to see them score. So by the middle of the first half, they were already yelling at our coach: "Why don't you let somebody else shoot!?" "Get that Earvin kid out of there!" "Make that Johnson boy give up the basketball!"

It got nasty. Even though their kids never said anything, the parents were going nuts. I started to feel badly about it, so I started passing the basketball to other guys. Then if they didn't score, I'd stand underneath *our* basket, grab the rebound, then put it back. That way everybody was happy because I began thinking that if I scored all the points then nobody else would have anything to talk about after the game. Everybody likes to brag about what they did, how many points they scored, things like that; so it made me think about the game in a different way. We were happy when we won, but everybody was even happier if they had gotten a piece of the action. That's when I started thinking about the importance of passing, about how I could still be involved in the entire game even if I wasn't shooting.

I became a passer in elementary school so that the other guys could score and be happy, and I haven't stopped thinking that way. Now, nothing makes me happier than walking into the Lakers locker room after the game and seeing a group of happy guys. Whether I scored 40 points or 4, if everybody's happy, then it means we won.

I'm not naive enough to think all twelve players are going to be smiling after every game. There are never enough shots or enough points to go around. But I try to remind guys that there'll always be another night, and sooner or later every player will get his turn. I remember early in Byron Scott's career when he would get frustrated because the offensive system the coaches designed revolved around other players, usually Kareem. He'd try to keep his feelings inside, but you could see it in his face. He was frustrated and sometimes felt as if maybe he didn't belong in the NBA. Our lockers are across the room from each other, so I could always see the look in his eyes. I tried to tell him to hang in there, but for the most part players have to learn to deal with those kinds of things themselves. Fortunately for us, Byron was patient enough to wait his turn. By 1987 he was our leading scorer and one of the most dangerous guards in the league. It was a crime that he always got overlooked when it came to be selected to the all-star team, but what made it worse was that I felt he was overlooked because he was playing with me. That wasn't fair to him, and Byron never took it well when he was left off the team, but he never let it affect how hard he played for the Lakers, which was probably a very hard thing for him to do.

The challenge of trying to keep everyone balanced is what makes me think of passing as a great piece of art. It's like something you can hang in a museum and watch over and over again. You can put it on a stage and admire it like a great Broadway show. A great pass is a thing of beauty. It's a Picasso or a Rembrandt. Even when I see some of the guys I play against— Larry Bird, Mark Jackson, Maurice Cheeks, or John Stockton— something inside of me gives them a hand whenever they make a nice pass. Sure all artists compete, but they can also admire each other's creations. That's the way I am when it comes to passing, and other players who like to pass feel the same.

That's part of the reason why Larry Bird and I became such good friends and great admirers of each other's game. The first time I saw him play in person was on the day of the semifinals of the NCAA tournament in 1969, the year our two teams played for the championship in Salt Lake City. I had heard about him but you can't judge a player until you see him in person. Let me go on the record now as saying Larry Bird was every- thing he was built up to be. This guy was *bad*. He took an average Indiana State team and just *would not let them lose*. Whatever it took, Bird did it. Whether it was scoring, rebound- ing, or passing, he was there. Against De Paul in the semifinals, he hit ten straight shots during one point in the second half. He was unbelievable.

At practice the next day, our coach Jud Heathcote had a sur- prise for us, especially me. Instead of having the whole first team practice together like we normally did, he told me to join the second team. I was a little confused for a minute, but then he told the starters, "Men, this is Larry Bird. Double team him as soon as he puts the ball on the floor. Harass him, surround him, cut off every possible passing lane."

Jud knew that Bird was a great shooter, but he believed he could hurt you more with his passing because a great passer can keep a team off balance. The opposing team has to be concerned about everyone on the floor because it doesn't know who's going to get the ball at any given time. He turned to me and said, "Be Bird."

I had a blast that day; I pulled out all my tricks. I made passes from everywhere, took shots from any part of the floor. I even took a few hook shots from deep in the corner. I was being Bird, all right, trying to do anything and everything that he would against us. It drove my teammates crazy, but by the end of the day, Larry couldn't have done anything against us that we hadn't already seen.

At tip-off the following day, I was as psyched for a game as I ever was in my life. I was playing for the national championship, but I was also playing against Larry Bird.

Larry and I have shared a lot of things in our careers, but what we've respected most in each other was that we both loved to pass the basketball. And we loved to win.

Passing may be an artistic part of the game, but it also took a lot of practice and hard work, with my mind and my body. To become a truly *great* passer, I had to learn to give up a lot. I gave up thinking like a scorer. Everybody loves to score so they can get all the attention. They can look in the stands and yell, "Hey, Mom! I scored!" That's great. But great passers give up all of that. I gave up the glory and the cheers because even when my pass results in 2 points, most fans are cheering for the person who made the shot. I compare it to being the director of a play or movie. Chances are if people enjoyed the show, they go home and talk about the actors, the music, or maybe the scenery. But it is directors who see that actors speak their lines with the right moods, that the lighting director lights the stage just right, and that the set designer has the proper scenery and the costume designer the correct clothing; directors watch over everything so it is just right. Directors know how important their roles are to the success of the play, as do actors and everybody else who works on the play, but they usually get overlooked by the audience.

Fortunately, for me and other passers, that's changed a lot in pro basketball, and I'd like to think I had something to do with it. Of course, I didn't *start* passing as an art. There've been

I consider passing to be an art. Here I look straight ahead to freeze my defender, then look left to Kareem.

plenty of players in the past who were recognized as great passing artists. Probably the best was Bob Cousy.

The first time I saw an old tape of Bob playing with the Celtics, I said, "Wow!" He was coming down the floor making no-look passes, dribbling between his legs, and doing all the fancy stuff we thought we invented on the playground when we were imitating Marques Haynes. Then there were players like Lenny Wilkens and Nate (Tiny) Archibald.

People even forget that some of the league's top scorers were also great passers. Wilt Chamberlain averaged more than 30 points per game over fourteen seasons, but he also liked to pass and did it often, sometimes just to show people that he wasn't greedy about scoring. And even though Oscar Robertson, the Big O, scored enough points to become the game's fourth all-time leading scorer, he also managed to pass for more assists than any player in history. His 9887 assists is the goal I'm chasing. If all goes well and I don't have any major injuries, I should reach Oscar sometime near the end of the 1990–91 season. Keep your fingers crossed! It would be a great honor to catch the Big O, my way of paying tribute to all the great passers who came before me.

Great passers are like directors of plays because their job is setting up the offense so that the other guys can score. They set their teammates up for *their* shots instead of looking for their own. I enjoy that because I'm making the game move to *my* beat. And all players love the passer because the passer helps them score.

Timing is everything when it comes to passing, and you can't waste time trying to decide what type of pass to use in different situations. On the basketball court, I have to make decisions in a split second—the chest pass? the bounce pass? the overhead pass? the outlet pass? the overhand pass? the baseball pass? the wraparound pass? Then comes the execution, and it's all got to be as quick and smooth as a cat darting after a bird. It's not instinct, though. That "natural" ability comes from practice, lots of it.

I know that all my passes aren't perfect, but to come as close as possible, I told myself at an early age that I could never make enough passes in drills or at practice. I figured if I made 1000 bounce passes every day, pretty soon I'd know just how much power and spin to put on the ball to make it go where I wanted it to. That's why I spent innumerable hours working on different passes. I even work on the no-looks that look as if I created them on the spot. Chances are that anything you see me do during a game I've done 1000 times in practice. And it's worth every minute I put in before, during, and after practice because I get such a thrill out of getting an assist or making a great pass. I've made plenty of passes during my NBA career, too many to single out the best or most important one. But my two most memorable passes involved Kareem Abdul-Jabbar.

In the spring of 1985, when Kareem was closing in on the all-time scoring record, I made it clear that I wanted to make the pass that led to the record-breaking point. You can never time those things down to the exact moment, but we wanted to give it a try. It really wasn't too hard to keep track because during those last few days reporters from all over the country started to follow the team around. They were as anxious as we were to see the historic moment. Finally, going into a game against the Utah Jazz on April 5, Kareem was so close that we knew it was going to happen that night.

I told everybody: *That assist is mine!* I told the coaches to keep track so we'd know when his next shot would set the mark. It turned out that it wasn't necessary because the closer he got, the more the crowd in Las Vegas, where the Jazz play some of their games, got into it. Here we were in a hostile arena, and they were cheering every time Kareem scored. It was great.

Finally, it seemed as if everyone in the world knew Kareem's next basket would be the big one, so we ran what was our bread-and-butter play—just me feeding Kareem in the low post from outside with everybody else on the other side of the floor. It's called a two-man game with two defenders against two offensive players.

The defenders were Rickey Green, who was guarding me, and Mark Eaton, the Jazz's giant center. Mark has had some good games against us, but this time he didn't have a chance. I floated a soft one-handed pass over Green's head. Kareem caught the ball, faked a couple of times, then spun around for his patented skyhook from about 15 feet out. It was dead on target, and the place went wild. It was a great moment, one I'm glad I can tell my kids I was a part of.

An almost exact replay came at the All-Star Game in Chicago in 1987 when Kareem was on the verge of breaking the all-star scoring record. We were both on the bench near the end of the game, and it looked like neither one of us was going back in.

Every pass requires split-second decision making and complete concentration.

But the crowd started chanting: "We want Kareem! We want Kareem!" Pat Riley, who was coaching the West team, usually doesn't get affected by anything the crowds do. But the chant got louder and louder, so Pat turned around and looked at Kareem like, "Well, Cap?" Kareem said, "Why not?" I knew I was going in, too, because I wasn't going to let Kareem break a record without me. So we went back in and ran the same play. Just like in Salt Lake City, the place went wild when Kareem made the skyhook after catching my pass. Once again, I've got something to tell my grandkids.

Now to make great passes, I have to see the whole floor. One of my campers once said to me, "But, Mr. Johnson, I've only got two eyes!" To me, that's not true. I think I have about 100 eyes all over my head. Some of them are in the back; others are on the side or behind my ears. I just had to train myself to use all those eyes.

For instance, I'll take that same camper down the floor with me on the fast break. OK, here we go. First, we've got to look behind us to see if someone's trying to catch up to us and flick the ball away. Now we've got to look around in both directions. We've got to look at all the players on defense and see who's fast and who's slow and where they are on the floor. Are they in front of us? Are they alongside us? We've also got to check out our teammates. Who's where? Who's in the best position to shoot? To rebound? To set a screen? Who's covering our teammates? Are there any mismatches? Who's free? Who's quick? Who's slow? Who can make the shot? Who can block the shot? Where are the passing lanes? The cracks? The seams? Now, who's going to see all that with just two eyes?

From what I've seen, I'm not the only one with all those eyes. Everywhere I go, whether to a gym in Los Angeles or to a playground in my hometown, I see players who love to pass. It makes me proud, but what makes me most happy is that players are becoming smarter. I see guys moving the ball around the outside of the defense—the perimeter—looking for an easy shot. They know how to read a three-on-one fast break and which guy to pass it to. They know how to pass, and they want to pass. That makes me feel good because it's as though I helped start something.

I'm always asked about which players I emulated when I was younger. Well, I tried to take a little bit from everybody— Dave Bing, Jerry West, Oscar Robertson, Wilt Chamberlain. There

Utah plays some of the best team defense in the league, so it takes team concentration to beat them.

was at least one thing about all those players that I tried to put into my game.

I just liked Wilt. There was the size factor and what he could do. He could shoot, rebound, and pass. People always focus on his scoring, but they forget that he also led the league in assists and rebounds. Wilt could do what he wanted. In trying to do everything well, I really tried to imitate him.

Oscar also affected the way I approach the game. To him the basketball was a science to be studied. He wasn't fancy; he just did the work and reaped the rewards.

Jerry was cool. He was the guy the Lakers depended on to take the big shot, and he didn't back away. All great players are like that, but I remember Jerry because he hit so many game-winning shots that he seemed to have the market on being Mr. Clutch.

Back in my neighborhood in East Lansing, everybody wanted to shoot the Dave Bing Jumper. At the playground down the street from my house, guys came down the court and said, ''Bing!'' even if they didn't shoot like him.

As I got through the first five years or so of my career, I began reading about how different guys patterned themselves after me, and it felt good. After having the respect of your peers, that's the ultimate compliment a player can have, to have guys imitating them on the playground.

Mark Jackson was one guy who talked about playing like me, and I can see some of myself in him. He plays the game up high as I do, with his back straight as though he wants everybody to know he's in control. People think he's slow, but he's not; it's just his style. His smarts are more important than his overall skills. His showmanship—everything except the finger-waving and airplane routines he goes into after scoring a big basket—and floor leadership are a lot like mine. But he doesn't try to be too fancy, and he doesn't make a lot of turnovers. When Mark is on the floor, you know the game is in his hands.

The last segment of the passing game involves what might seem like homework: getting to know your teammates. It's important for me to know everything I can about the guys I'm playing with because one little bit of knowledge might make a big difference in the outcome of a game. For instance, I have to know exactly where everybody on the Lakers likes to catch the ball and how good they are at catching certain kinds of passes.

I knew Kareem always wanted the perfect pass right where he could catch it without leaving the down-low spot he worked so hard to establish. If he had to go get it, he wouldn't. So I had to be very careful.

James Worthy is quick and has good hands; he can catch the ball almost anywhere. He'll give me signals that tell me where he wants the ball. He likes to catch it and make his move quickly, so I have to know whether he wants it high or low or as he makes his move.

A. C. Green doesn't catch the ball well in traffic, so there's no use even giving it to him in that situation. But then Mychal Thompson has great hands. He's one of the few big men who can catch the ball on the break and not commit a turnover.

Knowing these kinds of things keeps me from making the wrong decision and, ultimately, helps me become the kind of confident passer and floor leader that will help my team be as good as it can.

Here are some drills that I still use and explanations of the different types of passes. Sound footwork is the basis for all of them, and you want to put your whole body behind the pass. Start with your legs by stepping through every pass with whichever foot you feel most comfortable. If you're right-handed, it's usually your right foot. In your mind, think step, then release. Step, release.

Chest pass: This is the basic basketball pass, the pass you'll see used more than any other kind. If you want to work on this, stand face to face with your friend and about 10 feet apart. Grab the ball with both hands level on either side and hold it to your chest. Now, take one step while pushing the ball away from you. Your elbows come up and out, your fingers come behind the ball, and you follow through by pushing all the way through the ends of your fingers. That's so you can get all your power behind the pass. Repeat the drill with your friend until you're zipping passes between yourselves, but not so hard that your friend gets hurt or can't catch the ball. That defeats the whole purpose of the pass.

Bounce pass: With this pass, you're bouncing the ball off the floor to get it to your teammate around the defensive man in front of you or when you're trying to get the ball through traffic to a teammate in the lane. You want the ball to come to your teammate anywhere between the navel and chest. If you keep the ball in that area, your teammate can handle it easily and can do whatever he wants to with it. It's the most valuable pass because it can get you out of a lot of jams. But it also requires more practice because you've got to know where the ball's going to go after you pass it. So again, stand face to face with your friend. Now use the same motion that you used making the chest pass, only aim the ball to the floor. Step and release. Remember always step through the pass just as you do to follow through when you shoot.

Overhead pass: Being 6'–9", I use this pass a lot. Because I'm usually taller than the player defending me, I can see over him. By holding the ball above my head with both hands, I can get a lot of leverage behind the pass. This is the pass I use when I'm trying to get the ball to Kareem or James in the low post. When we're playing the two-man game, it's the safest, most accurate way to pass the ball into the post if the player wants the ball up high. Just like the bounce and chest passes, step through when you release the ball.

Baseball pass: This is where we get to pretend we're baseball or football players. We're the center fielder trying to throw the runner out at home plate. Or we're the quarterback trying to hit the receiver streaking down the sidelines and going for the touchdown. Either way, this is the pass you'll use when you're trying to make a long, high pass to a teammate who is usually at the other end of the court. You might use this pass when you're inbounding the ball after your opponent has scored. The Lakers' strategy is to get the ball out of the net as quickly as possible, then look for a teammate breaking away from the pack across midcourt. To get the ball to him with enough velocity and height to get over and past the defense, you have to throw the ball like a center fielder or quarterback.

With your partner, practice this pass as though you were passing the football around the backyard. Holding the ball in both hands, pivot, turn toward your friend who's running the other way, and then try to get the ball to him. The step and follow-through is just like the other passes.

Outlet pass: The outlet pass might be the most important pass in basketball. It's the pass that comes when your teammate has gotten the rebound and the flow of the game starts the other way. What happens in the next moment will probably decide whether your team gets an easy basket or not. A good outlet passer will snatch the ball off the glass, look over his shoulder, find the open man, and get the ball to his teammate all in one

*I always wanted to play center field; step in-
to it and follow through.*

motion. A great outlet passer can also see the whole floor. In that same instant, he'll look to see if there's anyone running to the other end of the floor who's open; if so, he'll make the pass—usually an overhead pass—to the open man and then just sit back and watch as his teammate goes in for the easy 2 points.

The outlet pass is different from the other passes for two reasons. First, you've usually had to turn completely around before you can pass the ball. Second, because you usually have at least one, if not more than one, defender surrounding you, you're trying to get the ball through traffic to your teammate. A good outlet passer has to be both strong and decisive.

There's nothing like watching a great outlet passer at work. Two of the best ever were Wes Unseld and Darryl Dawkins. Wes was a great position rebounder, and he was usually always in the right place when it came to getting the boards. Both guys were strong passers who could read the whole floor instantly. Darryl was so strong it was scary. When he threw the ball, he made it look so easy that it did look as if he was throwing a baseball. Wes was more of a traditional outlet passer, a guy who made the pass with two hands over his head. His technique is what I try to teach in my camps. When those two players were in their prime, if you were the other team, you knew you had to get back quickly on defense or you were going to be reading the backs of the other team's jerseys all night.

Kareem was also a great outlet passer. At 7'–2", he could usually see over the defense and whip a baseball pass down the floor so fast that we always had an advantage at the offensive end. If we didn't score, Kareem would join us at the offensive end, and then we would run our half-court offense. People used to criticize him for not getting back on offense quickly, but most of the time Kareem had already done his job by getting the ball and getting it to the right man so we could score.

To practice this pass, have your friend take a shot. Now rebound the ball with both hands. Then as you're coming to the floor, look for your friend and try to get the ball to him as quickly as possible. Sometimes, he'll be in the corner or at the top of the key; other times, he'll be at midcourt or running toward the other basket. Tell your friend to let you know where he is by yelling your name. During games, that signal can only help you make the quick pass.

You can also practice by yourself by placing several chairs in different spots on the floor and using them as targets. Throw the ball off the backboard, get the rebound, turn, and fire.

One final thing when it comes to passing: If you're playing with me, you always have to be on your toes and on the lookout for the ball because I may try a pass at any time to anybody. It's really embarrassing when you get thumped in the head with the ball because you weren't looking for the pass.

Rebounding is hard work, especially when I go up against a bigger, stronger player like Utah's Mark Eaton.

5

Hard Work:
Rebounding

My ideal rebounder is the biggest, the meanest, and the strongest player on my team. That's who I want underneath the boards when the game is in the final seconds, the opposing team is down by 1 point, and they've just missed a shot. That's because rebounding is the ugliest part of the game.

A player has to have heart, desire, and a strong body to be a good rebounder. He must stay down low with his knees bent for balance and use his rear end to box out his opponent. He has to keep his body between his opponent and the basket at all costs, then explode to the ball.

Height doesn't mean anything when it comes to rebounding. Charles Barkley is listed as being 6'–6'' when he's probably only 6'–4'', but he's one of the meanest rebounders in the game. That's because he's got the heart and the desire to go after the boards, no matter where he is on the floor or who's trying to block him out, especially if it's a big rebound at the end of a game. If that's the case, then you'd better look out for Charles because he's going to be somewhere near the basketball. I just hate to see him when the teams go out for warm-ups because I know it's going to be a long night's work. Another player like that is Fat Lever. He's a 6'–4'' guard for the Denver Nuggets, and he's also their best rebounder. A 6'–4'' guard? Heart and desire.

For most young players, probably the hardest thing to master in basketball is the ability to maintain that desire. Rebounding isn't glamorous. It's not considered *Showtime!* (even though *Showtime!* would be *Slowtime!* without strong rebounders). How many players like Moses Malone, Akeem Olajuwon, Buck Williams, and Karl Malone are out there? Those guys want the ball every time it goes up, and they know how to get it. They know the fundamentals and the tricks of the trade. They know the dirty part of the game, and they love it.

I confess: I didn't like rebounding when I was younger. Nobody did. Because I was taller than most kids my age in elementary and junior high school, rebounding was easy. But as I got older, the guys starting getting bigger, and rebounding became less fun and more hard work, the hardest kind of work there is. But one thing I've heard from every coach I've played for, the key to every victory is rebounding. Sometimes it's how well you shoot and pass the ball. It's usually how well you play defense, but it's *always* how well you rebound.

When you hear that enough, it finally sinks in. I learned in high school when Coach Fox made two things about rebounding very clear: If we don't rebound, we don't win; and if we don't rebound, we don't play. That was all a bunch of high school players needed to hear. Anything that took from their playing time was going to be taken care of quick.

Even now with the Lakers, Pat Riley is always talking about rebounding. It's his pet peeve. Whenever we lose, it's usually because we didn't get the best effort on the boards. I don't mean we didn't *get* enough rebounds, just that we didn't get the *effort*.

With five players jumping and moving in different directions on the floor, people might think it's hard for a coach to see who's giving their best effort at all times. Not Pat. He and his coaches have a grading system that breaks down the game into several categories. One is "rebound effort." It doesn't tell them whether you *got* the rebound but whether you *tried* to get the rebound. To the coaches, it's the effort that's most important; you can't always get the rebound, but you won't ever get it if you don't go after it. Assistant Coaches Bill Bertka and Randy Phund rewatch tapes of every game and grade every player in every category. The results are usually for the coaches. They use them to make various adjustments in the lineup, like the breakdown of playing time. But when it's necessary, a player will hear about his grades if he has been slacking off in any category.

At first, nobody liked the idea. Who would? We all thought we stopped getting grades back in college. But after a while, we started to realize that grades helped because sometimes a player might be doing something unconsciously. Maybe he'll be going to the wrong place on plays, playing too far away from his man, forgetting to set a strong enough pick, or not going after rebounds. Every coach will tell you about those things, but it's not always easy for the player to accept what the coach is trying to tell him. With the grades, there's no argument. It's all there in black and white.

The effort needed to be a good rebounder is helped by having the knowledge of how to be a good rebounder. That means knowing how to anticipate which side of the basket certain shots will go to, how to establish a good inside position against the player who's your responsibility, and how to hold the player back, then explode to the ball. If it's an offensive rebound, the job is a lot harder; chances are that the defensive player was already closer to the basket when the shot went off, and so it's easier for him to get the inside position. In that case, I refuse to accept the box-out, spin out of his grasp, plant my feet, and then explode.

When I was young, I didn't think rebounding was something you had to work on, like passing and shooting. On the playground, the best rebounders were the guys who never quit. If they had to jump three, four, or five times to get the ball, they would. Moses Malone reminds me of those types of guys. He's only 6'-10", short for an NBA center. He doesn't have long arms, and I've never seen him jump really high. But as long as the ball's in the air, Moses will have a chance to get it. He joined the Atlanta Hawks before the 1988–89 season and was the main reason that they became contenders that year. They were a good team before he signed his first huge contract with them, but he brought them a toughness, both mental and physical, they didn't have before.

Moses works harder than most guys in the league, always has, especially on the offensive end of the floor. He's strong and quick, which enables him to hold his ground against bigger guys, as well as beat them to the ball. Moses is also smart. Because he prides himself on rebounding, he took the time to learn how different shots will react to the rim.

For instance, a rebound from a shot from long range will probably bounce off the rim hard. Shots from the corners usually skip to the other side. You can also tell that Moses knows how all

While battling Larry Bird for a rebound, I use anticipation, position, and determination to win the contest. At least this one.

his teammates shoot. He knows those who shoot line drives and how they bounce straight back. And he knows that those who shoot high, arching shots will have rebounds that stay close to the rim. He can also read a shot better than almost anybody. He can tell if it's going to be short or long or whether it's going to bounce off to one side or the other. Getting all that knowledge is part of being a great rebounder, and it's what has always made Moses one of the most dangerous players in the league.

In 1981 at the end of my second year in the pros, the Lakers played the Houston Rockets in the first round of the play-offs. We were the defending champions, and we had the best record in the league. The Rockets barely made the play-offs and were 40–42 during the regular season. It was a best-of-three series with games one and three at our place, the Forum in Los Angeles. Of course, we were confident, but we were having problems, too. We weren't used to playing the role of champions, and we let the pressure of defending the title change the way we approached the game. Instead of being a team, we became twelve individuals, which is the worst thing that can happen in basketball. We had a complete team breakdown. Besides that, Moses wore us out. He was everywhere, grabbing every rebound, beating us down the floor on the break, and blocking shots. And he's the kind of guy who inspires his teammates. Pretty soon, they were all playing as hard as Moses. He was setting the standard for the whole team. It was over when I missed a short jumper at the buzzer in game three. We lost by 1 point and lost the series 2–1. Missing that shot is still one of the low points of my career. But even if I'd made it, we couldn't have taken anything away from Moses. He carried the Rockets all the way to the finals that year. Houston took Boston to six games before losing, but people still try to say the team was a fluke because of its regular-season record. But any team with Moses Malone on it is not a fluke.

Rebounding is probably the most passionate part of basketball. It's emotion; it's heart. When six or seven players are battling for the ball, it can get vicious underneath the boards. Sometimes, it makes players do things they otherwise wouldn't. Tempers get out of hand, and people become something different from what they really are. They take cheap shots or just start taunting somebody on the other team. That usually leads to the fights everybody hates to see. They're just an instant reaction to the emotions on the floor, mainly around the basket. All

Because Larry and I are such good friends,
neither one of us wants to give an inch.

players wish there was a way to stop the fights, but I don't know if there is. As long as guys are trying to keep their jobs and trying to win championships, things always have a chance of getting out of control.

Learning to be a good rebounder is a matter of wanting to be a good rebounder. When I'm practicing by myself and want to work on that part of my game, I use one main drill, one that's part rebounding, part conditioning. I start by taking a shot that'll bounce off the rim. Then I charge after the ball and snatch it down. I quickly put it back up so that it comes off the rim again, then jump and grab it again. I go for as long and as hard as I can. I don't think about anything except getting the ball off the rim and putting it back up. When I'm playing one on one after practice with one of my teammates, I also use the game to work on blocking out. We don't usually go all-out in those games, but the blocking-out techniques—playing defense, getting inside position, then holding your man off the boards—can be practiced at any speed, and the benefits will come when you need them, such as when you need to be the best rebounder on the floor.

My last line of defense is to block my man's shot, then hope for the best.

6

Takin'
Your Best Shot

Swish! I love making that sound. When you
shoot the basketball and it goes—Swish!—as it slips through the
net, that's the sweetest sound of all. And of all basketball skills,
shooting is the one perfect combination of every element. It
takes different skills, technique, timing, and execution. It's putting all elements of basketball together for the ultimate reward: 2
points.

Everybody who's ever played the game loves to shoot, and
I'm no exception. But it may not be your role on the team to
shoot all the time. I went through that for the first seven seasons
of my career with the Lakers. During all that time, people just
assumed I couldn't shoot. Most everybody said that Larry Bird
was a much better shooter than I was, and that bothered me. I
told my friends that none of those people had ever seen the
"real" Earvin. I hadn't been turned loose yet because that wasn't
my role. On those Lakers teams, Kareem Abdul-Jabbar, Norm
Nixon, and Jamaal Wilkes were the first options of all our plays.
Kareem held the inside, Norm took care of the outside, and
Jamaal had everything in between. They were the players who
were turned loose to shoot anytime they wanted, while my job
was to set them up. I was the director; they were the stars.

I understood my role and didn't have to deviate from it just
to show everybody that I could shoot. That would have been

silly, and it would have affected everything we were trying to do. And it probably would have gotten me a seat on the bench.

That all changed in the summer of 1986 when I got a letter from Coach Pat Riley. As I've said before, he sends letters to every player outlining their off-season conditioning program and telling the player what kind of goals he should be setting for the next season. The letters are well received because they get you thinking in the right direction when you might be down emotionally about what happened the season before or too high from winning it all. What Pat told me that summer was simple: He wanted me to go for it.

Pat had decided that it was time to start changing how the Lakers played the game, how we used our weapons. He wanted me to become the primary scorer. He wanted me to be The Man. As I read the letter, I just about jumped out of the room. Finally, I was going to be able to show everybody what I could do. Finally, I was going to be able to play *my* game. But right then I got concerned. I was worried about what Kareem might think. He was The Man on the Lakers from the day he arrived from Milwaukee—June 16, 1975—after the most important trade in Lakers' history. He *was* the Lakers, not me, not Norm, nor anyone else. When I think about the original Lakers in Los Angeles, I think of Jerry West, Elgin Baylor, and Wilt Chamberlain. But when I think about the second generation, I only think of one man, Kareem Abdul-Jabbar. Now, just like that, Pat Riley wanted to change all that.

Because the last thing any team needs is tension among players, I wanted to speak with Kareem as soon as possible. We were still going to depend on him, especially in the clutch when we needed a critical basket to win a game or a championship, and I wanted to make that clear.

When I finally reached him—it was weeks before training camp was supposed to start—Kareem surprised me. He was always a generally quiet man, sometimes hard to read even though he was as open with his teammates as he was with almost anyone. But I didn't know how he'd react to this kid taking over the main scoring responsibilities. From the start, he made me feel comfortable about the change. He said that he understood and that he'd still play a key role on the team. That's just what I wanted to hear.

When we got to training camp in the fall, everyone talked about it again, but by then it was settled. Riley said he was making the change to make the Lakers more of a running team again. He wanted to make us less predictable and hoped we'd become comfortable attacking teams from every position. He said that's why he was giving the ball to me.

Looking back, I'd have to say that the 1986–87 season was the most fun I'd ever had. It was hard work for me, more so mentally because suddenly I was looking for my own shot as much as I was looking out for everyone else. It was just the opposite of the way I'd played for my entire life, so it was a big change. But it worked. I had my best overall season in the NBA. I scored almost 24 points a game and increased my assists, rebounds, steals, and blocked shots. During the play-offs, I also learned I had been voted the Most Valuable Player for the first time in my career. I was truly honored, but when I received the award I couldn't do anything but dedicate the trophy to my father. He's the reason I'm on this earth. Both of my MVP trophies belong to him.

During 1986–87, even though my scoring average went up, my shooting percentage stayed about the same as it was in my previous year. Throughout my career, I've made just over half of my shots, which isn't bad for a guard. But because I was scoring more, all of a sudden people were saying, "Oh, he must've worked on his shooting during the off season," or "I didn't know Magic could shoot!" When I heard those things, I just stood there, shrugged, and said, "Oh, well." What *can* you do?

I guess people failed to watch game six of the 1980 finals in Philadelphia when I was a rookie. Before that game, everybody said that we couldn't win because Kareem was at home with a sprained ankle. We were up three games to two and needed just one more win for the championship, but people just wrote us off. They just assumed there was going to be a game seven, and that upset us. We all thought to ourselves, "Well, if that's the case, maybe we shouldn't even play. Why did we even come here?" No one said we could win, but we knew we'd have at least one advantage, psychological. Maybe the 76ers didn't think we could win either, which basically made us the underdog.

In sports the underdog always has the advantage because the favorite must cope with the pressure of having to win when they're *supposed* to win. We had the home court for the series, so we were favored to win the whole thing. But on that one night we were the underdog, so we had the advantage because no one expected us to pull it off—except us. And we did.

Coach Pat Riley looks on approvingly (I think) as I put up a long jumper from the corner.

The worst part was that Kareem had to watch his team win the championship from his home in Los Angeles. I think we made it up to him before he retired. The game turned out to be the best single game of my career—42 points, 15 rebounds, and 7 assists. It'll probably be my best ever. Everything was clicking, and I was just rolling with the emotions and adrenaline that were building up inside. The juices were flowing because of what was at stake. It was as though I was in another world. I felt like I could do anything. I didn't care who was playing defense against me or what the situation was; I was going to make *something* happen. But it was also one of the strangest games I ever played. I started the game by jumping center, but when we started playing, I didn't play inside like a "normal" center. Instead, I stayed outside and shot jumpers. Caldwell Jones, the 76ers' center, was guarding me, but he gave me the outside shot all night. I guess the word among the 76ers was that I couldn't shoot, and they just decided to let me stay outside as long as I wanted. I finished the game with 42 points. That's still the second-highest total of my career. I know that I've always had the ability to shoot; maybe nobody was watching.

That game was completely different from most of the games during the first seven years of my career. With Kareem, Jamaal, and Norm dominating the offense, I had to enjoy most of my scoring highlights during practice. The only thing that kept me from losing confidence in my shooting touch during those early seasons was that the guys on the team played H-O-R-S-E every day in practice.

That's right, just like we used to on our playgrounds and in our driveways. It's still a great game for developing and maintaining your shooting skills, as long as you take it seriously. And when the games came down to me, Byron Scott, and Michael Cooper, we were nothing but serious. We didn't play around shooting lay-ups, either. All our shots were long-range, deep, and in the corners, sometimes even from the seats.

Byron gets crazy when we play H-O-R-S-E. He's usually the first one to set up from somewhere in the stands. The problem is that he usually makes them! He usually wins, but winning's not the main point because no matter who wins, everybody's gotten in some good shooting practice.

We played that game almost every day for seven years, so when the coach finally gave me the ball, I was ready. Most fans, even those who'd been watching the Lakers forever, didn't know what I could do as a scorer; so in a lot of ways, I felt like I was proving myself all over again.

If there was one part of my shooting where I didn't have the confidence during most of those early seasons, it was when I had to take the last shot in a close, critical game. A lot of players are like that. Basketball is easy in the first quarter when everybody's rolling because there's not any pressure. But in the fourth quarter, the rim suddenly shrinks, and those same guys that were burning it in the first half suddenly don't want to shoot or they just don't have the touch like they did in the first three quarters. Basically, they don't want the big shot, and there's a reason for that.

Everything that happens for most of the game is almost like playground games. Everybody tries to make their shots, but if you don't, you know there's plenty of time to recover. That's not the game in the fourth quarter. With under 3 minutes left and the score closer than 10 points, every shot matters. You almost *have* to score on every possession and you have to stop the other team from scoring. Defensive pressure is a team responsibility, and scoring the big basket usually takes the cooperation of everybody on the floor. But *taking* that shot is an individual job, a job not every player is willing to take.

When you square up, aim for the rim, and release the basketball, all eyes are on you, and the outcome of the whole game is in your hands. Some players like that; others would rather be on the bench. On the early Lakers teams, Kareem, Jamaal, and Norm all wanted the big shot. But when my turn came, I wasn't ready. I was scared to go for it because for so many years I wasn't *the* guy. I wasn't used to those situations. I didn't mind if I was at the free throw line with the chance to win it or if I grabbed an offensive rebound and got the shot that way. But to just set up the offense and take the jump shot? No way. Usually in those situations, Kareem was the first option, Jamaal was second, and Norm third. I just got crumbs, but that was cool; that's all I wanted. But that attitude finally caught up with me in 1984 when I experienced the low points in my career during the championship series against Boston.

It began at the end of game two in Boston Garden. It looked as if we had the game won with a 2-point lead and the ball with just seconds left. But James Worthy's inbounds pass to me was stolen by Gerald Henderson, and he scored an easy lay-up to tie the score. I should have come to the ball, so that was

I always try to kiss the ball off the glass when shooting a lay-up.

mostly my fault, not James's. Then he tried to set for a final shot, but I just didn't know what to do. I'd never been in that situation before, and I just blanked out. Dennis Johnson was all over me, and before I knew it, the clock ran out. A victory in that game would have given us a 2–0 lead going back to Los Angeles, so there would have been almost no way we could have lost the title. But we lost the game in overtime, 124–121.

We had another chance to take a two-game lead in the series at the end of game five when we had the ball with 16 seconds left and the score tied 116–116. We set up a two-man isolation play with James in the low post and me out on the wing. Kareem had fouled out, so Robert Parish was able to guard James. Parish is over 7'; James is 6'-9". I have to admit that what happened in game two was still fresh in my mind, so I was trying to be extra careful with the ball. I was too careful. I dribbled for about 10 seconds, then tried to lob the ball to James. But the pass wasn't strong enough—Remember when I told you to step, plant, and follow through with your passes? Well, I didn't, and Parish was able to use his height advantage to reach around James and flick the ball away.

Then in overtime, I choked again. I'm a good free throw shooter, 82 percent over my career and 81 percent in the play-offs, which means I don't get affected a lot by the pressure of the postseason. But with the score tied again, 123–123, I missed two shots from the line with 35 seconds left. Two! Bird then scored, and we threw away the inbounds pass to lose the game. Now instead of being ahead three games to one, the series was tied 2–2. The Celtics eventually won in seven games.

I'm not ashamed to admit that I lost that series. Now I can say that's exactly what happened. The next few months were the worst summer of my life. Now I think of that as one championship we don't have, and I feel it was my fault. That's why I still feel badly about it years later, even though we've won three championships since then. It was the lowest point in my career. No question about it.

It took me a long time to accept being wrong, but I finally did. I accepted failure and promised myself that I wouldn't let it happen again. That's when I really learned that I could deal with a lot of adversity. A lot of players would put something like that off on somebody else. Give it to me now in those situations, and I've got the confidence to make the right decisions.

This was the biggest shot of my career—I hit the "junior" skyhook to defeat the Celtics in game 4 of the 1987 NBA finals on Boston's hallowed parquet floor.

When I think about my biggest shot, there's no doubt that it came in game four of the 1987 finals against Boston. We were leading two games to one, but the Celtics were up by 1 point with less than 10 seconds left. Sound familiar? Well, this time I took the ball, and I knew exactly what I was going to do. Parish was guarding Kareem inside, and I was being guarded by Kevin McHale on the outside. I knew I could get around Kevin, but I had no idea what I was going to do when I did. So I started to drive.

McHale was right with me, and then Parish jumped out to help. Suddenly my mind went clear: the skyhook. Well, really, it was what I called the junior, junior, junior skyhook because nobody but Kareem can really shoot the skyhook. I had asked him to teach it to me, and we'd been working it out for a long time, maybe a couple of years. But I'd never felt comfortable enough with it to use it in a game. Once you get the steps and the timing of the skyhook down, it's a great shot. It's all timing and footwork. And it absolutely can't be blocked!

Unlike most shots where once you've started your motion you're committed to the range and height of the shot, you can make midair adjustments with the hook shot. That's what I had to do when I saw Parish coming over to help out. Seeing him made me put a little more arch on the ball to get it over the two guys' hands. It was one of those situations that went in slow motion. When the ball went through the net, all you could hear was about fifteen guys screaming their heads off. Other than that, it was silent inside Boston Garden, which is one of the best sounds I'll ever hear.

When it comes to shooting the hook shot, Kareem is the master. I just added it to my game because I needed something else, another shot down in the low post. When I first approached Kareem about teaching it to me, he was surprised. No one had ever asked him about it before. But I figured anything that helped him play in the league for so long had to work for someone else, so I thought I'd give it a try. The first couple of times I tried it, I was really clumsy. It's different from any other shot because you don't square your shoulders toward the basket and shoot the ball with the traditional release and follow-through. Instead, you gather yourself with your back to the basket, set your feet correctly, then execute the shot over your shoulder, catching a glimpse of the rim as you're "hooking" the ball into the sky. A

Without my left-handed shot, I never would have made my elementary school team, not to mention the NBA.

flick of the wrist can give the shot more or less of an arch, depending on how the defense is playing you.

Every player should learn the skyhook because it's versatile and can be used in any situation. It doesn't matter if you've got a bigger or a smaller man covering. The key is the follow-through. No matter what position your body's in, the follow-through has to be the same every time. That's the secret. I try to teach the shot to all the older kids at my camps. If you learn the hook, you'll be something different, something special.

Shooting Instructions

Everybody loves to score. When I was little, everybody who scored looked up in the stands, waved to mom and dad, and yelled, "Look at me, I scored!" Well, before you can do that, you have to start with the basics. These are some of the techniques and drills I use when I want to work on my shooting.

When I think about my *jump shot,* I always start with my footwork. I have to get my feet far enough apart so that I'm balanced. For me, that's about shoulder's width. Some players need a wider stance; others keep their feet closer together— whatever feels comfortable.

Moving up the body, I make sure that my knees are bent, again comfortably but enough so that I've got a good base, which allows me to explode into my shot.

I'm right-handed, so whenever I shoot a jumper, I want to make sure my elbow is bent at a 45-degree angle with my triceps perfectly parallel to the floor when I'm prepared to shoot. That helps me keep my hands up and gives me a base to follow through.

When I'm ready, I balance the shot with my left hand on the side of the ball, which keeps it on line with the basket. I aim and follow through with my right hand and arm fully extended. I also try to follow the ball through the net with my eyes and hands. That helps me remember to follow through.

I try to keep my shoulders square to the basket, too. That's why it's so important that my feet are square to the basket be- cause they make sure the rest of my body follows. Consistency is the key to good shooting. Every time I take a jumper, I want it to look like all my other jumpers. Once I develop that consistency, I can maintain it even when I'm being bumped and pushed by a defender.

*Even when I'm taking a jump shot between
two defenders, I try to use perfect form—
knees bent, shooting arm at a 45-degree
angle, and triceps parallel to the floor.*

To develop that consistency, I play a game called Around-the-World. In it I take jump shots from designated spots on the floor. Starting on the low box on the right side of the basket, I bank a short jumper off the glass. Then I'll move to the midway point of the side of the lane and shoot again. Next I'll move to the corner of the lane, then to the free throw line, and finally around the other side until I'm shooting the short bank shot from the left side. All the while, I'm running to get the rebound and hustling back to my spot on the rotation. I do this until I hit all seven shots, both going and coming without a miss. I'll add shots from both baselines, and then a shot from the top of the key. Finally, I can add any spot on the floor as long as I've worked myself "around the world" without missing a shot.

I try to teach kids to be comfortable about using the glass, the backboard. That glass is the shooter's best friend. I even gave it a name; I call it "Suzy." When I'm going to use the glass, I'll think "Kiss Suzy" to myself, then I'll kiss it off the glass.

The *free throw* is supposed to be the easiest shot in the game; that's why it's called "free." But it also can be one of the toughest. A lot of players fight their free throws because it seems so different psychologically. First, the entire game is stopped just so you can take that shot. During play you might miss, but with everybody running around and back and forth, there's no time to think about it. But on the free throw line, everybody's eyes are on you, and you just can't hide if you miss. Then, of course, the later the game gets, the more pressure the player has to deal with on the line; there are a lot of players who simply can't handle that pressure.

One of my worst missed free throws was because I didn't deal with the pressure well. It came against—who else?—Boston when they beat us for the championship in 1984. I wasn't used to having to deliver for us in those situations, and when I had to hit some big free throws down the stretch in game five, I couldn't. It was just a bad game for me overall, but I learned from it. The next season we came back and beat them for the championship in Boston, probably the Lakers' most important championship in the history of the franchise. In 1988–89, I shocked a lot of people—including myself—by winning the league's free throw title. It wasn't something I even thought about until well into the season when someone mentioned that I was near the top of the list. From that point on, I just let my confidence take over. Every time I stepped to the line, I thought I was

Concentrate, bend the elbow, follow through and—hopefully—swish!

going to make the shots. Because it was something new, winning the free throw title was as much a thrill for me as winning my second MVP Award. Well, almost.

My ritual at the free throw line is simple. Once I get a comfortable stance with my feet, again, shoulder-width apart, I'm ready. I bend my elbow and shoot the shot with the same follow-through technique I use on the jump shot. Some players get really complicated on the line. Adrian Dantley caresses the basketball, finds a particular spot, then rotates the ball until it fits into his hand just right. Dennis Johnson used to bounce the ball once for every year he was in the league. Once he passed the thirteen-year mark, he started bouncing it only three times—for his jersey number—because everyone was starting to get bored while waiting for him to shoot.

Another shot people take for granted is the *lay-up*. As simple as it is, you'd be surprised how many NBA players have trouble with it. Maybe the shot is too easy, but it's worth practicing as much as any other shot, especially using both hands. Being able to make a left-handed lay-up undoubtedly helps a player somewhere during his career. I've already told you how it helped me in junior high on the first day of practice. I could've been the best player in the gym, but if I couldn't make a left-handed lay-up, I would've been off the team just like that.

The key to the lay-up is concentration. Because the shot is taken so close to the rim, players tend to look away too early or take it for granted that the shot will go in. But no matter whether it's an uncontested breakaway or a drive through heavy traffic, I find a spot on the glass and focus on it all the way through the shot. There is nothing that can sway me from putting the ball where I want to—in the basket.

It doesn't hurt to watch the players who are some of the best pure shooters in basketball: Larry Bird, Jeff Malone, Dale Ellis, and my teammate, Byron. They've all got one thing in common. They're always ready to shoot, and when the ball comes to them, there's no hesitation, no second guessing. And they watch the ball all the way into the basket. What you see is the result of years in the backyard or on the playground just shooting alone. I must have shot two or three hours every day when I was a kid, either in the driveway or the park. That's when I had the chance to really work and develop my range.

When young players are starting out, I tell them not to try to shoot from far out. They should start in close where they can

Never take the lay-up for granted. You always have to concentrate and be ready for the rebound.

work on shooting the correct way until they're strong enough to shoot free throws with the proper form. At this stage, it's also better to play Around-the-World rather than H-O-R-S-E because players shouldn't experiment too much with fancy, long-range shots until they have the basic jumpers from short range down correctly and consistently.

Oops! I guess anybody can get caught in the air by a head fake from Kevin McHale.

7

Doin' It with "D"

There are three keys to winning basketball games: defense, defense, defense. It doesn't matter whether the level is high school, college, or the pros; championships are won with defense. From my high school state championship team in East Lansing to Michigan State and through five Lakers' championship teams, the focus of attention was always on our flashy playing style, our fast break: "Showtime!" as it is called in Los Angeles. But all those teams have one thing in common, and it isn't "Showtime!" It is *"Worktime!"*—even at the playground.

When my friends and I got together at the park for an afternoon of serious basketball, a lot of the guys didn't come to play a lot of defense. The other captains picked guys who could light up the scoreboard. They took the fancy scorers, guys who could dunk. But I believed that if you put five fancy names together on a playground team everyone played for themselves, not the team. So when it was my turn to choose, I picked the workers.

I took the guys who always got overlooked—the guys who liked to crash the boards and play defense until they were soaked with sweat. They didn't worry about how many points they scored, only whether their team won. Sometimes I'd take a guy who couldn't even dribble. The other captain would look at me as if I were crazy, but I knew something about my player that he didn't: He would do anything to win. And at our playground, just like playgrounds everywhere, it's all about winning, about bragging rights.

Every coach I ever played for stressed defense *ahead* of offense. Coach Fox at East Lansing High School filled more than half of every practice with defensive drills. His favorite was one the players hated most: a simple shuffling drill where players get in their defensive stance—feet spread, knees bent, hands out, and head up—at one corner of the free throw line, then shuffle back and forth along the line for 30 seconds as fast as they could. If somebody didn't go full speed, he had to get back in the front of the line and run the drill again, this time from one side of the *entire court* to the other. After doing the shuffling drills all week, playing good, solid defense during our games was a piece of cake. Besides, we didn't dare get lazy during games because we were always thinking about that drill somewhere in the back of our minds.

You have to really *want* to play defense. You have to really want to double team, rotate to the open man, and pressure your man for the length of the floor. But defense is truly the thinking man's side of the game. Great defensive players are always, always ready to react, always aware of their responsibilities, and never break the team's overall defensive scheme. They're never caught flying mindlessly all over the floor.

Centers Mark Eaton and Akeem Olajuwon rarely go for head and shoulder fakes or ball fakes when you drive against them. Akeem is so quick that he'll even switch defensive assignments with a guard and help cover smaller guys like Dale Ellis and my teammate Byron Scott.

Some of the toughest players who ever covered me are Dennis Johnson, Paul Pressey, Rodney McCray, Maurice Cheeks, and, of course, Michael Jordan. I'll hardly ever catch any of those guys leaning the wrong way where they can't react at any moment to any of my quickest moves. They know that if they have to think about it—"Well, if he does this, then I'll go there"—I'm gone. So they're always in a balanced stance with their feet wide apart, and I have to really drive hard to get around them, which I can't always do. And they're always in great position to react to the other players on my team.

They may not always block my shot or steal the ball, but they're always there to disturb me and maybe force me into making a move or trying a pass I didn't want to make. They're in my face all the time, especially during critical possessions or when they know for which of my teammates the play is designed. So

No, this is not a game of one-on-one, but
whenever I go against Dennis Johnson, one
of the best defensive players in the
business, it seems like we always have our
own "inner game" going on.

against these players, I have to use *all* my moves. I know I have to be almost perfect on offense, or they'll embarrass me. I win some, and they win some; that's basketball. That's also why they're all-league defensive players.

Coach Fox rewarded guys who played good defense with more playing time, as did Jud Heathcote at Michigan State. And nothing makes Pat Riley happier than a solid defensive game. Not everybody on the team is going to have the same amount of skills; but defense isn't only about skills, it's also about desire.

I wanted to be a good defensive player before I became a good defensive player. When Michael Jordan won the MVP Award in 1988 after leading the league in scoring with a 35-point average, he said he was happier about winning defensive player of the year that same year. Defense is where he proved himself; it was the reason he was MVP.

The Lakers' overall defensive strategy doesn't change much from season to season, except for small parts of it that can shift because there are different players every year. We've gone through a lot of roster changes since I arrived in 1979. So many players have come and gone that I think we could form another team with ex-Lakers—I'd take Jamaal Wilkes, Jim Chones, Mitch Kupchak, Norm Nixon, and Bob McAdoo for starters—and probably win a championship. But no matter who was here, one thing didn't change. Every year, despite all the changes, we improved defensively. We've gone from being just a good defensive team during the early years of my career to being one of the best defensive teams in the league. If you look at the top of the standings, you'll always see the Lakers among the league leaders in team defense, which measures how well one team stops its opponents from scoring. We also do pretty well in blocked shots, the dirty work again, which means our big men are helping out the guards when we get beaten to the middle of the floor.

But the real test is defensive-shooting percentage. In the NBA, with all of its great shooters, if you can force teams into hitting only about 46 percent of their shots, then you're working hard on defense and it's paying off. Detroit's always up there in most of those categories, too, as are New York, Cleveland, Seattle, and, especially, Utah. All those teams have guards who are tough around the perimeter of the defense, with forwards and centers who block shots.

The Chicago Bulls' Michael Jordan is one of the toughest defenders against me. Or anybody else.

Against New York, if you get past Mark Jackson, you have to deal with Patrick Ewing. In Cleveland, if you get by Ron Harper, you have to deal with Larry Nance. In Seattle, if you get by Nate McMillen, you have to deal with Xavier McDaniel and Alton Lister. And in Utah, if you get by John Stockton, you have to deal with Karl Malone and Mark Eaton.

Eaton is 7'–4'' and he seems like all arms. Just by being on the floor, he makes you twist and turn and try anything in midair just to keep him from blocking your shot, and he still blocks it.

When the Jazz took the Lakers to seven games in 1988 in the Western conference finals, it was primarily due to Eaton's defense. He may not score much, but he's unquestionably one of the most valuable players in the league. In 1988–89, he was voted the league's best defensive player by the media in the closest vote in the history of the award, which proves that when it comes to defense, almost everybody in the NBA is getting into the act.

Back at Michigan State, everybody talked about Magic Johnson versus Larry Bird being the key to the outcome of our game in the championship against Indiana State, but it was more about who played the best defense in the second half. We won because, even when our offense was struggling, our defense never dropped below the level at which we worked in practice. That's why we were able to maintain our lead during most of the second half. When we finally got it together on offense in the second half, we took over.

That's the reason why teams and players should never rely on dominating the opponent on the offensive end of the floor. Offensive skills come and go. Some nights the rim seems like it's as wide as a swimming pool. Other nights it looks like the head of a pin. But there's no excuse for inconsistency on defense because defense is effort and the effort should be consistently at the same level every night. On defense, there are no days off.

If defense is the key to winning, then the keys to defense are practice, preparation, desire, and one most essential ingredient: intensity. I know I have to be intense but not out of control on the defensive end of the floor. I also know I have to be balanced at all times. If not, then whoever I'm defending will fake me out of my shoes. To stay balanced, I have to stay low and try to beat my man to whatever spot on the floor he wants to go. Doing that comes from all those thousands of shuffling drills Coach Fox,

Coach Heathcote, and Coach Riley have been making me do for all these years.

When we play the Celtics, it's my goal to stop Dennis Johnson from scoring. But I know the *team* concept might call for me to double team Bird when he has the ball or to rotate to another man when we're trying to trap the other team. Executing the coach's defensive philosophy is just as important as playing my own man one on one. In the pros, players are so good that you just can't stop them by yourself, one on one, on a consistent basis, even though that's your goal. If I'm doing my job of playing good team defense and Dennis Johnson scores because he was open, there's nothing I can do about it, except try just as hard the next time the Celtics get the ball.

You almost always need help on defense. That's why you see NBA teams double teaming, rotating, and running traps and maneuvers like that almost every night. It's how we survive. In college, teams that play pressure defense with arms and bodies all over the court will rarely get blown out, even by a better opponent, because their defense keeps them close.

Sometimes I see kids in a game who are shy about asking for help on defense, or it's a macho thing. "Yo baby, you can't score on me." That type of talk. Well, not only am I not afraid to ask for help; on defense but I also *want* help; I look for it. Sometimes I even beg for it. When I'm staring Michael Jordan in the eye, it's not a good time to be shy or macho. If I'm out there trying to handle him by myself and I'm too selfish to alert my teammates when he's gotten by me, hey, that's 2 points. How macho is that?

Now, there are some great individual defensive players, and it won't hurt anybody to try and become as tough defensively as players like Michael Cooper, Sidney Moncrief, Alvin Robertson, or Michael Jordan—guys you just hate to see coming out for the opening tap and saying, "I've got you."

But not even those guys can stop players like Larry Bird, Charles Barkley, James Worthy, and Jordan themselves because offensive players always have a slight advantage. Offensive players already know where they're going to go, what they're going to do, and when they're going to do it. If there's just one man to beat, nine times out of ten they'll score. In baseball, a .100 batting average will get you another profession.

Playing solid defense is a challenge I look forward to every time I step on the floor. Containing my man or making the key

Whenever I'm double teamed, it means somebody's open. This time I found him, even over the outstretched arms of Derek Harper and James Donaldson.

defensive play makes me just as happy as scoring the winning basket. Well, almost. To the greatest defenders of all time—that includes players like Nate Thurmond, Jerry Sloan, Dave Cowans, Bobby Jones, and Kareem Abdul-Jabbar—stopping their man was like a slam dunk to a scorer, an assist to a point guard, or a rebound to a power forward. It's the same thing. I know Michael Cooper gets so excited when he gets a big stop that he gets everybody on our team and in the arena fired up.

A lot of players get confused on what defense means. I call their attitude the I-Got-Mine theory, and it's dangerous. The first thing these guys do when they get into the locker room is look at the boxscore. If their man scored big, they'll look at their numbers and say, "Hey, I got mine." But how many shots did they take to get those points? And did their team win? If the player didn't make any steals or create enough turnovers, so what that he outscored his man when his team didn't win? On defense, the guy staring at the boxscore might've been the player of whom the other team took advantage. That's macho?

Coaches watch us when we're playing defense more than any other time in the game, and any laziness will always show up in the stats. They look at field-goal percentage, steals, and turnovers for both teams. If the Lakers didn't outplay the opponents in those categories, chances are we were outplayed in another category, too—the score.

One of the things that bothers the Lakers most is that so many people refuse to give us credit for being a good defensive team. For a long time, all we ever heard about was "Showtime!" When we got ready to run our fast break, it was "Showtime!" Nothing else we did mattered to a lot of people, but we've never won a championship with offense alone. We're sound defensive players who play good team defense, especially in the play-offs.

We've always had a few standout individual defensive players—Jamaal Wilkes, Coop, Kareem, and Norm Nixon, guys like that. But our strength has always been a well-conceived and well-executed defensive scheme, anchored by Kareem and complemented by my "lunch-pail" guys like Jim Chones, who played on my first championship team in 1980; Kurt Rambis, who played a major role in our championships in 1982, 1985, and 1987; and A. C. Green, who started on our back-to-back championship teams in 1987 and 1988.

Players like that choke up the lane and harass people all night. I like to double team and sneak around on defense when I think I can anticipate what the opposing team is going to do. Kareem was always helping out and blocking shots just as they teach you in the seventh grade. We always knew that you sold tickets with offense, but won rings with defense.

The Stance

I can always tell when it's in the final minutes of a tight game. Players on both teams are more focused and more intense, especially on defense. That's when guys are crouched in the perfect defensive stance when their man has the basketball, and all attention in the arena is focused on them. There's no hiding, and any mental mistakes can be not only costly but also embarrassing.

As I said, the offensive player always has the advantage because he already knows what he's going to do and when. So he'll always have that split-second jump on the defensive players, which means the defender has to be in perfect position—feet spread more than shoulder's width apart, knees bent, rear end low, arms out—to make up for that disadvantage. The defender's center of gravity should be perfectly even, so his weight should be evenly distributed on the soles of his feet. If his weight is too far forward, he might land on his face. Too far back, and he might find himself on his butt.

When defending someone near the top of the key, the defender should keep both feet squarely placed toward his opponent. That will change depending on how he wants the offensive player to react. By placing one foot slightly ahead of the other and offering the offensive player an opening in one direction, he can force the offensive player in any direction. Usually, he's sending him into the middle, into the lane, where there are defenders who'll help out when he gets past the first man. Sometimes defenses are oriented toward the baseline, which means players will try to force their men into the other direction. Or, if a player simply doesn't drive well toward one direction or the other, then the defender will try to force him toward that weaker side.

The best defensive players balance themselves with their arms at their sides, slightly bent at the elbow, and hands relaxed. They keep their heads up and eyes focused on the offensive player's chest. Too many players try to stare down the guy they're guarding. Well, that's the worst thing they can do.

Defenders who do that are usually the ones getting blown away by a head-and-shoulders fake. The chest is the only place players can't fake. Anywhere they're going to go, that part of the body is going with them; solid defenders will always watch the chest.

I also try to be aware of what's going on behind me. Peripheral vision is important in every phase of the game but even more so when I'm playing defense. There's nothing worse than running into a blind pick at full speed; it's like running into a wall you can't see. The biggest challenge on defense is to always be aware of at least two things: the offensive man and the ball. That's especially tough when I'm covering someone on the weak side, the side opposite of where the ball is. With the rest of the action on the other part of the floor, I have to move around until I find a position where I won't have a blind spot. Sometimes that just won't happen, so I have to depend on my teammates to let me know what's happening. I also have to be more alert because one of the most embarrassing plays in basketball comes when you get beaten backdoor or when your man gets a lay-up because, with the ball on the other side of the floor, you were lulled into thinking he wasn't part of the play. If you can see your man and the ball at all times, that won't happen.

Aggressive "D"

Just because the Lakers don't have the basketball doesn't mean we have to wait for the other team to make something happen. Defense can be the start of good things if it's played aggressively. We want to disrupt whatever they're trying to run. It wouldn't be unusual for us to have one of our guards apply pressure to whomever is bringing the ball up the court. From the stands that might look like wasted energy because the defensive player rarely makes the steal, but that's not why we do it.

When I have Dennis Johnson in my face for two hours, it takes a lot out of me. He applies pressure as I bring the ball up the floor in the first half, so that maybe I'll be just a little bit tired in the second half. Applying pressure to the ball handler makes him waste valuable seconds, so that when he crosses the 10-second line his team has that much less time to run its plays before the 24-second clock expires.

In 1984 when I made those plays against the Celtics in the finals that cost us the title, I may not have been physically tired, but I was mentally drained from having to deal with Dennis all afternoon. He had accomplished his goal.

Nobody said dunking would be easy, even against an old teammate, Kurt Rambis.

There are other tactics I like to use to try and disrupt an offensive player. If I know a guy's a jump shooter, I simply stay in his face and never give him room. I never let him get into a rhythm. Players like Byron Scott on our team, Dale Ellis in Seattle, Danny Ainge, and Jeff Malone—all the best shooters—are at their best when everything is in sync. The Lakers didn't want to let that happen. So we were told to belly up to the jump shooter, even if it meant being called for a foul early in the game. By being there, I've let the guy know that it's going to be a long evening and that no matter what I'm not going away. Later on, maybe he'll be looking for me rather than the ball or the basket.

Just because an offensive player is about to shoot doesn't mean the defender has run out of options. If I've played against the player, before long I probably know his shooting habits, his routine. Does he bring the ball low before he shoots? To his waist? To the side? Every player has a routine that helps him get into his shooting rhythm. If I haven't played the guy before, I use the first few minutes to try to figure out what he likes to do best; then later I might be able to flick the ball away as he starts to coil for the shot. If I'm really in tune with his rhythm, I might be able to block the shot, but that's probably the toughest aspect of playing defense.

It's too easy to hit a player on the arm and get called for the foul when you're reaching up. Blocking the shot is my last resort. It's more important for me to stay in the game than to block any shot, unless it's the last one in the final seconds of a close game. But even then, I'm always careful. It's also too easy to get faked out of my sneakers and end up being embarrassed twice—because the guy went to the free throw line for the winning shots and because I ended up on my tail.

An aggressive defender shouldn't be afraid to use his hands. Hand checking is illegal in colleges and the pros, but it's still an effective defensive tool if the defender is smart. Sometimes a gentle nudge can throw off a shooter's timing. Or, if a player has already driven around you, a nudge might disrupt his balance just enough to create a turnover or disrupt his concentration. Back before hand checking was outlawed, defenders literally grabbed the offensive man and were able to move him where they wanted him to go. Some players still try to hand check players. When I'm being defended like that, it definitely affects how I can maneuver around the court, and it hurts.

Reggie Theus, formerly of the Kings, hand checks me in the stomach, an illegal but effective and widely used tactic to throw off a player's balance.

Finally, when I'm double teaming an offensive player, I do it aggressively. Being timid only allows the player time to see what I'm about to do and make an adjustment. When I get the guy, I apply as much body pressure as the referees will allow. I keep my arms up for balance and to deflect desperation passes. Then after all that work, when a teammate and I have clamped a player down with a serious double team, all that preparation, practice, and hard work have finally paid off.

Weak-Side Defense

It's easy to get lost out there or to relax. But weak-side defense is as crucial as playing defense against the player with the ball handler because in most instances the guy with the ball will be looking for someone to pass it to and that's usually somebody on the weak side.

Defenses are so sophisticated these days that they try to create double teaming situations that cause every player to rotate toward the player with the basketball. That leaves someone open, usually the man farthest away from the ball. Teams will either swing the ball quickly to get it to the open man or try to rifle the pass over the defense before it has a chance to relax. The player who's the last line of defense for his team has to be especially aware of where that weak-side player is at all times.

The secret to playing defense away from the ball is being aware of where the ball is. If I'm in a man-to-man defense, I try not to let my man get away from me. If the play is designed for him, he'll be moving through screens and picks trying to get rid of me. Usually, I've already tried to discover the best path that will keep me in between the player and the basketball but close enough to the player to disrupt his shot if he does get the basketball. Sometimes that path will be over the top of the pick—in front of the screen—rather than behind it. Either way, I try not to get rattled if I'm not right on his shoulder, as long as I'm between him and the player looking to pass to him.

Many times, if I follow the player behind the screen, it gives him just the split second he needs to catch a pass and get his shot off. Dale Ellis is a player with that kind of quick release. The Lakers have tried all kinds of defensive schemes to keep him from getting into the flow that can explode on a team. One trick the Lakers use is to keep a player on his shooting hand at all times, whether it's the player guarding him or someone who's had to switch onto him. Dale likes to catch the ball and shoot it in one motion; if we can get someone on his hand for an instant, it's usually enough to throw him off.

During the play-offs at the end of the 1988–89 season, we tried a different twist. Because at 6'–6", Dale is slightly taller than Byron Scott, who normally guards him for us, Pat Riley decided to make a switch. He placed James Worthy, who's 6'–9", on Ellis during almost all of our second-round series. James plays forward for us, but because of his quickness and agility he can play almost anywhere. We swept the Sonics in four straight games, largely because Ellis *never* found a rhythm. He was frustrated by James.

James's work against Dale was a great individual effort, but it took place within our team concept—one where we try to overload the strong side of the floor with defenders, which forces a team to make several passes to get an open shot. Some teams try and call it a zone, but in the NBA, zone defenses are illegal. What we do is a combination of zone principles and man-to-man responsibilities, which gives me more things to think about and be aware of than I had in college. It's as if you're playing a zone and a man-to-man at the same time. It's even more important to have an eye focused on the entire floor, but particularly the area that's yours. It's confusing, but it's the only way to play.

Whistles

Fouls are a part of the game, so I don't let them discourage me. I even try to learn how to use them to my advantage. The most important thing is not to get into foul trouble—I can't play if I'm on the bench. But I'm never afraid to "waste" a foul early in the game if it means making a point to the guy I'm guarding. I may want to tell Joe Dumars of the Pistons, "Hey, nothing's gonna be easy today." By making him know I'm there early, maybe he'll start thinking about me more than his shot. Later on in the game, I won't commit that same silly foul because I've already accomplished what I intended to do.

Sometimes fouls are unavoidable. If the offensive man has dribbled around the defense and the only options are to allow 2 sure points or foul the player, most coaches don't get upset when you commit the foul. But there's a fine line between committing a "silly" foul and a "smart" foul.

When time's almost run out on the shot clock, you don't want to foul someone who's taking a jump shot from long range.

That's a low-percentage shot, lower than a free throw, a lay-up, or a dunk. Or, if the Lakers are ahead by 1 point in the final seconds and the opposition is in the bonus—meaning they'll shoot two free throws no matter who's fouled—we want to do everything we can to play good defense without committing a foul.

Drills

Basketball isn't ballet, but it's close. Most of what happens on the court is the result of footwork. Good footwork will always keep you in position to make the play. You won't be off balance, and you won't be forced into situations where you've lost control because your feet wouldn't go where you wanted them to go. I've already said that you have to train your body to react the right way without having to think about it. You do that by completing defensive drills over and over again until your feet begin thinking on their own.

The Lakers still use these drills. When we come to training camp every fall, it's just as it was in high school. The drills are boring, and they hurt. But it's what we have to do to reach our potential as a team. We know it's not just the talent we have but the little things we do during training camp and practices that make us contenders every year. Hard work in the fall will pay off in the spring.

Here's how we do it:

1. **Lateral step:** Take the defensive stance at some point along the sideline. Now move to your right, keeping both feet on the sideline as you move in one direction, then the other. Move around the entire court, remembering to keep your knees bent, hands and back low. When you reach the point where you began, start in the other direction, this time a little quicker, until you've reached point A again. Make four complete trips around the floor, with the last trip being as fast as you can move without getting your feet tangled up.

2. **Backpeddling:** When the opposition is running the break, you've got to backpeddle until they commit the play in one direction or another. Start at the free throw line with your back toward the opposite end of the floor, just as you would if you were shooting a free throw. Begin by running backward for three or four quick strides, then turn either left or right as if you're reacting to the fast break. Sprint to the other baseline facing the

sideline as if you're running alongside a player who is bringing the basketball up the floor. In my camps, we run this drill with one defensive player against two offensive players. The offensive players don't commit themselves until the last moment, which means the defensive player must keep changing directions until one of the player commits to shoot.

3.   *Changing directions:* In this drill, you're trying to make the offensive player change directions with his dribble, as if you're pressuring him from one end of the floor to the other. Staying as close to the dribbler as possible without committing a foul, overplay him to one side until he changes direction with the basketball. Then overplay him to the other side until he changes directions again. Repeat this all the way down the floor, back and forth.

I talk to my teammates and signal with my hands to set up a play, especially when I'm in an All-Star game with guys I hardly play with.

8

Talkin' Trash

*T*hey say talk is cheap. Not so on the basketball court. Communication in basketball is as important as anything else that happens out there, from playing defense to blocking out underneath the boards or trying to score the winning basket. Talking is just more subtle.

From the stands, most fans don't know if there's any talking taking place on the court or not, unless the players are really obvious. Spectators don't see or hear the jawing unless two players from opposite teams really start mouthing off to each other. By then even the people in the cheapest seats know what's going on.

On the Lakers, Michael Cooper is the real talker. Most of the players pretty much keep their thoughts to themselves on the floor, everyone except Coop. Most nights, he starts talking to guys on the other team from the moment he comes into the game until the final buzzer, sometimes even during the warm ups. Most of the guys we play against know him already, so he doesn't bother them, but that's not why he does it. Coop does it for motivation. As a matter of fact, the more he's talking trash, the better he plays.

But there's another kind of talk, and that's called communicating with my teammates, even if it's only by using a sign language we've developed through the years. Even way back at East Lansing high school, we had signs that we used when we were out on the floor. The arenas were usually very noisy whenever we played, and it was hard to hear each other. The easiest way of communicating is with eye contact. It's also the easiest way to disguise what you're about to do.

All James Worthy has to do is look toward the ceiling by rolling his eyes, and I know he wants the alley-oop pass on the fast-break or back-door play. I can also look at Byron's eyes and tell which way he's going to come off a screen because we've worked out different signals during practice. That little bit of communication gives us just enough of a split-second advantage over our defenders to turn the play into a basket before the defense can react.

Most people seem surprised to learn that communication on the court can make or break every play. They think it's all instinct and reaction, with players simply running around playing ball without any strategy or game plan. The truth is that every possession has a plan all its own, for both teams' offense and defense. What determines which plan works is execution, and the key to proper execution is usually communication.

Communication is especially important when the other team has the ball. Just as an offensive player has an advantage because he knows what he's going to do before the defensive player does, the team with the ball has an advantage because not only do they know the play that's been called but they also know all options that come with that play. With all the sophisticated scouting and coaching in the NBA, teams usually know each other's plays pretty well. Still, it's up to the defense to throw a blanket around the play, and there's no way players can do that without communicating.

Take, for example, the pick-and-roll play. When Mychal Thompson and I are defending against two offensive players running the pick-and-roll, we talk ourselves through the different options even as the play is developing. That way we don't end up in the same place at the same time, which would leave somebody open for an easy lay-up or jump shot. Because he's defending the player setting the screen, let's say, Portland's Kevin Duckworth, Mychal keeps himself between Duckworth and the basket. From this point, he's like the center fielder in baseball. Whatever we're going to do, it's his call. I'm concentrating on my man—against Portland that would be guard Terry Porter—trying to fight around Duckworth's screen. Terry's got the ball, so he's also got control. First, he'll dribble by Duckworth, who'll then roll to the basket and wait to see what happens next.

If I get picked off by Kevin and Mychal doesn't react quickly enough, Terry'll probably take the open jumper. If Mychal jumps out quickly, leaving me guarding the Blazers' 7'–1'', 240-pound center, then Terry will try to loft a pass over Thompson and allow Kevin to take advantage of the mismatch underneath.

To stop the play, Mychal has to tell me from what direction the screen's coming. Because he can see all three players, he's able to see the play develop before I do. I'm trusting him to tell me what's going on with a simple "Screen left!" or "Screen right!" I also have to know whether we're going to switch defensively, whether we're going to stay with our own man, or whether we're going to double team the player with the ball, no matter whether it's Porter or Duckworth. Sometimes what we do depends on the strategy devised by the coaches, but if Mychal doesn't communicate with me during the play, then we'll probably trip over each other and end up on the floor embarrassed.

Most of the time, the strategy during plays like that has already been designed by the coach. When great one-on-one players like Isiah Thomas and Michael Jordan run the pick-and-roll, Pat Riley usually tells us to double team them quickly; that way they'll have to give up the ball. When Larry Bird or I run the play, teams don't like to double team us too much because we'll always try to find the open man. When we have the basketball out high, near the top of the 3-point circle, there's a lot of space for us to work with, a lot of openings we can create, so teams don't double team us very much that far away from the basket.

When Bird runs the pick-and-roll play with Robert Parish, the Celtics center, it looks just like the way it's drawn on the blackboard. If the defense doubles Bird, he'll get it to Parish for what's usually an easy slam if the weakside defense doesn't react quick enough. If the defense doesn't double him, Bird will try to lose his man with a little fake, then nail the open jumper. He's such a great shooter there's usually not much you can do about Larry one-on-one. If the two players switch, they're dead because Parish will usually end up being guarded by a smaller player and Bird will get the ball to him for another easy 2 points.

Whenever we're on defense, I try to keep my teammates alert about what's happening on parts of the floor they may not be able to see. They do the same for me, especially the forwards and center because they're nearer the basket and have a view of the whole floor.

We usually have some idea what kinds of plays the other team likes to run, what their tendencies are, and the strengths and weaknesses of each individual player on that team. But by the time the game gets started, most of that knowledge is usually out the window. The other team had a scouting report, too; it all comes down to which team runs their plays, reacts, and communicates better.

Another key time for communication on the defense is when the other team is setting screens or picks from the blind side. If my teammates don't talk to me in those situations, I might not make it through the night. Once, I almost didn't.

During the first few years of my career, Wes Unseld was still playing center for the Washington Bullets. He's been retired since 1981, but he was still the hardest pick I ever ran into. I was a rookie, still untested and naïve when it came to things like that. Wes wasn't one of those tall, muscular centers. He was a wide double-thick brick wall. Wes was only 6'–7", short for a center, but he weighed almost 250 pounds! And it was solid rock, as I found out.

One night, he set a pick that nobody told me was coming, and I just went flat. I was chasing somebody up the floor, and the next thing I knew the lights went out. I crumpled to the floor as if I'd been shot by a sniper. My whole body went limp. The coaches and trainer came running out to the floor and asked me if I needed a 20-second time-out. I said, "Twenty seconds? I need a day's time-out!" When I got up, Wes just stood there smiling.

There was another time when I forgot to turn my head and look where I was going. That was a big mistake because Darryl Dawkins of the Philadelphia 76ers was there waiting for me. Darryl was 6'–11" and 250 pounds, as solid as granite. My body went one way before I looked where I was going, and— Wham!—I didn't see anything but different colors. By the time my head turned to look, I was already there, into a Dawkins wall. It's like seeing the train just before it smashes you in the face. My whole body shook. Everything hurt. I shudder now when I even think about it.

Getting knocked off by a blind pick will wake you up. It'll also make you angry. Once it happens to you, you'll let your teammates know you didn't appreciate being left in the dark. I've seen players almost start fights with their own teammates after

Sometimes you just have to plead your case.
But most of the time, you lose.

they shook off the effects of a blind pick. It's not right to get mad at the player setting the pick. He's just doing his job.

I've seen some guys knocked out completely by picks set by players like Dawkins, Karl Malone and Rick Mahorn. Mahorn, who was selected by Minnesota in the expansion draft following the playoffs, was at his worst during the first few years of his career when he played for the Washington Bullets and was teammates with Jeff Ruland. Everybody called them McFilthy and McNasty because they seemed to get so much pleasure out of seeing you in pain. I never knew which one was which, but it didn't matter.

In Detroit, Mahorn and Bill Laimbeer were once called The Bruise Brothers, but I still think of Mahorn as McFilthy. Or McNasty, whichever one he was. He and Ruland were bookend brick walls, and the Bullets ran me into them so many times that by the end of the evening my whole body was bruised and battered. You'd see Ruland out of the corner of your eye, but then you wouldn't see Rick. I once saw them just crush Michael Cooper, then smile at the poor guy as he was being helped off the floor. You never want to see that happen, but it's all part of the game.

Communicating on offense is important, too, but not so much with words as with signals. For me, that might mean moving my eyes in the direction I want my teammate to go or simply nodding my head. As the point guard, I usually call the plays, but it's my body language that tells my teammates what to do once the play begins.

When the Lakers have the ball, Byron Scott might have a lot of options for one play, but he'll use some sort of body language to say, "I'm going this way," or "I'm going that way." I've learned to read his signs by playing alongside him in the backcourt for several years. I can even tell how confident he is by the look in his eyes.

On nights when Byron's feeling good, I try to feed him the basketball as much as possible. On those other nights, or on any night when one of my teammates doesn't have his rhythm, I try to get them involved in ways other than just scoring. James Worthy and I almost have our own personal language now, especially when he's gotten down into the lane where I can dump it down to him quickly. He can either go toward the baseline or over the top of the defense. He might give me a signal with his finger that'll tell me whether he's going one way or the other. Then, in a flash, I make the pass and he's gone! It was the same with Kareem. I could tell by looking into his eyes—I guess I should say, through his goggles—whether he wanted the ball and what he was going to do with it. He lost some of that look early during the 1988–1989 season, his last season in the league. His game just wasn't working for him, and I think he was simply confused. Also, the team started to move more and more away from him out on the court. His incredible ten-year string of 787 games scoring in double figures had ended in Milwaukee on December 4, 1987. Now, about a year later, he was being criticized by the media as we came to town again. Near the beginning of his final season, two columnists in Los Angeles wrote that Kareem should retire rather than waiting until the end of the season. Even some of us got caught up in the Kareem-bashing hysteria. We started waving Kareem out of the way during plays rather than using him like we did for so many years. Here was the greatest center of all time, and we were waving him out of the way! To think of it now is embarrassing. Kareem was hurt, but he tried not to show it. It took a screaming session by Pat Riley to shock us back into reality. After that, there was no more bad-mouthing each other.

From then on, we were a different team. We were able to use Kareem for his strengths and not worry about his weaknesses. The man was forty-two years old at the end of his final season, the oldest player ever to play the game. He was a sports miracle, and we should have just appreciated him for that. Once we got past midseason, he started to feel good about himself again, and he was an important factor for us until the end of the season.

His biggest game of the season came when we needed him most, when the team was close to the brink of defeat against the Pistons in the championship series. It was game three, and the site was the Forum, our first appearance at home after losing the first two games of the series on the Pistons' home court. It was also our first game since I got hurt in game two, and everybody was wondering whether or not I could play. As it came close to tipoff, I tried everything I could in order to get ready. I had nursed and treated my hamstring with every remedy known to man, from stretching to electronic stimulation. I stretched for hours on the floor of the locker room, never once taking my mind off the task ahead. I worked and I worked. I even hoped that the adrenaline of the crowd and the game would make me forget the pain. But in the back of my mind, I knew I couldn't play effectively. I *hoped* I could play, and perhaps give the team a lift. But I knew the chances were slim. I started the game, but lasted only four minutes and 9 seconds before Pat took me off the floor. But my teammates didn't drop their heads. No one sulked. No one gave up. Especially Kareem.

We lost the game, 114–110, and fell three games down in the series, but not before Cap had his best game of the season. For one last afternoon, it was like old times for the Big Fella. He was skyhooking, rebounding, passing, anything and everything. He finished with 24 points and 13 rebounds. It was a performance that made me want to ask him to stay around myself. It was the best he could give, and everyone knew it. We'll all miss Kareem. So will the game.

The Lakers use our practice time to develop signals and get to know our teammates' playing habits. We've created a language among ourselves by developing certain strategies that might help us in certain situations and practicing them until they become second-nature. Remember, basketball isn't a one-man show. It's not darts or bowling. Nobody wins championships by themselves. It's a team game, and it doesn't do any good to waste practice time.

Lakers' practices are efficient and timed precisely by the coaches, almost to the minute. Coach Riley knows exactly what he wants us to accomplish every day. For the players, practice isn't a time to be cool or aloof. It's a time to work and study each other's playing habits. After a while, I knew every player's favorite spot on the floor. I knew Kareem liked the low post on the right side of the basket where he could work his man over by slowly backing him down, then burying the skyhook. Byron is a jump shooter, so he likes to get the ball out on the wing near the sidelines where he can either take the jumper or drive to the basket from about a 45-degree angle. Those are his strengths, and he's most confident when he can get one of those two shots, rather than something in between. James Worthy and A. C. Green are versatile. They can take the ball into the low post where they can use their quickness to beat the defensive player to the basket, or they can move just outside the lane where they'll face their man and drive around him off the dribble. Coop is another shooter who likes to "spot up" in one of his favorite areas of the floor. He's more a set-shot artist, whereas Byron's a classic jump shooter; Coop will just find a spot on the floor, usually behind

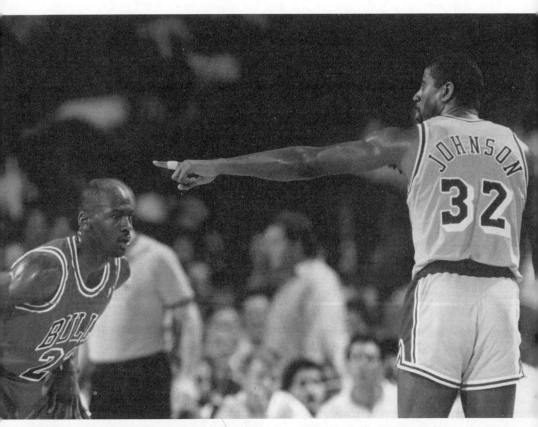

*It's my job to set up the attack. I take it
seriously, especially when the defense is anchored by Michael Jordan.*

the 3-point line, while all the other players are running around the court, then wait for someone to pass him the ball.

He was usually open because teams usually got so caught up in double teaming either James, Kareem, or me that they forgot about Coop. That's a mistake because he could kill a team from 3-point range every time, as just about everyone found out at one time or another.

Besides knowing where my teammates are most comfortable with the basketball, I also try to know where they're not comfortable. Learning these things takes time. When players and coaches talk about their team's "chemistry," they're usually talking about how well the players know each other and how well they get along more than they're talking about the players' skills.

The Lakers have great chemistry because we've been lucky to have the same nucleus of players for many seasons. Nothing's worse for a team than constant changes or players who don't want to sacrifice part of themselves in order to win. But even effort doesn't always make it happen.

In 1988 Orlando Woolridge joined our team from the New Jersey Nets. He came to us with a whole bunch of skills that nobody else had on the team. He was a leaper, somebody who could fly through the air after rebounds and lobs like Coop and James; but at 6'–9" and 215 pounds, he was bigger and stronger than either of those guys. He was big and quick like A. C., but much more agile, and explosive offensively. By the time he came to the Lakers, Orlando had already averaged 18 points in seven seasons with Chicago and the Nets. But it took all of us several months to get to know him and to understand what he could do, especially me. There were still some tough times. He struggled to fit in, and Coach Riley benched him for a string of games in the middle of the season. He always tried, but something seemed to be missing. There was no consistency to his contributions, even though his effort never changed. When a team reaches a certain level, there's not much of a margin for error; it was difficult to cope with Orlando's problems fitting in while coping with our own goals of trying to win our third straight championship. But the final product was worth it. When Coop and Woolridge were playing well, which finally started to happen at the end of the season and the playoffs, we had one of the strongest benches in the league. That became obvious in the first game of the Western conference finals against Phoenix when I had one of the worst games of my career. I was in foul trouble for most of the second half and finally fouled out with more than 3 minutes left in the game. Playing without me was a new situation for our team, but Orlando was one of the players who answered the call. He was tremendous in the fourth quarter in every phase of the game. Three days later, Orlando was a key player for us again as we took a 2–0 lead over Phoenix with a 101–95 victory in Los Angeles. He only played 14 minutes off the bench, but he scored 11 points and had 5 rebounds. Afterward, Pat didn't hesitate with reporters when they asked him how important Orlando had been to the team. He said, "Without Orlando, we don't win this game." On those two nights, Orlando Woolridge finally became a Laker.

Getting to know a new player doesn't happen overnight, but it's important if the team is going to become smooth and successful.

The way I look at my role as a floor leader is to remember that it's sometimes more important how you say things on the court than what you actually say. I'm always firm, especially in the late stages of the game, if one of my teammates is consistently in the wrong place. But I try not to order anybody around. Tensions can get pretty high on a basketball court, so I don't want to fan the flames. It only makes matters worse. Of course, sometimes I have to be tough. After all, Pat has given me the reins and the responsibility of running the team.

Generally, I just try to maintain an air of command. I'll call the plays. I'll praise and criticize guys when they need it. I'll tell somebody, "Hey, you've got to get here" or "That's not the play we want," rather than just yelling at them outright. Some guys are still hard-headed, so I've learned to know when to be forceful and when to be more gentle and how each guy will react to each tactic.

My role didn't change much as I played for different teams during my basketball life. At Michigan State, my job was just to get the ball to everybody. I had to distribute it because we had several scorers, players like Jay Vincent and Greg Kelser who could put up big numbers on any night and Don Bergovich and Terry Donnally who could shoot the ball from long range. With this group, I knew exactly what I had to do. Jay could hit the jumper from the top of the key all night, Greg played inside, Terry played along the baseline, and Don played the wing. It was a nice team because everybody was part of the action, everybody was into the flow, and everybody got their shots. That was the key: We were a close team and we complemented each other

*When I'm on the floor, I don't want there to
be any doubt about who's in charge.*

well. Over the years with the Lakers, nothing really changed, except a few of the faces, until I became more of a scorer in 1986. Even then, I never forgot that it was still my job to make everybody happy.

It's hard to explain how to become a leader. I don't believe you can just designate someone; leadership has to come naturally. I've always been one of the leaders on my teams, but not just because I was one of the best players. I think I always knew what it took to win. Some players simply play the game; others try to win the game. I always liked winning, no matter what kind of game it was, on any level, or what was on the line—a victory or a championship. Winning is winning, and to be a leader you have to understand that winning is more important than being the star. I know that any all-star in the league would trade that experience for an NBA title.

Just because I'm out of the game and sitting on the bench doesn't mean I'm not responsible for communicating with the guys on the floor. The worst thing I, and my teammates, can do is to not pay attention when we're on the bench.

When I was in high school, if anybody was caught fooling around on the bench, watching girls, or not helping the players out on the floor, they were gone. Coach Fox didn't tolerate that, and neither does any coach at any level. He said players who act like that don't have any respect for the importance of their role on the team; and if they didn't respect the role, then they should give it to someone who does. That changed my entire outlook. From then on, I realized that there are only twelve guys on a team. That's a pretty small group, so whether you play a lot of minutes or never take off your warm-ups, everyone on the team belongs to a pretty special group.

Through the years, the players on the end of the Lakers' bench haven't gained a lot of respect from people outside of the team, mainly fans. But the rest of us know they play an important role. They watch the game as intensely as Pat does because they know they have to know what's going on out on the court in order to step right into the flow, if they're needed, and help us out. If they're called on and haven't been watching, once they take the floor they just waste time trying to figure out what's going on. If they need 5 minutes to figure out who's playing well and who's not and what plays are working, they'll be back on the bench by then.

When my teammates get their chance to shine, it's my time to celebrate.

*When someone else makes a great play, I
want to be the first one to let them know it.*

The reserves should also watch from the bench because they can be another set of eyes and a valuable voice that can help the players on the floor. From their vantage point on the sideline, they can see things that players in the game can't because they're involved in the action. So with the Lakers it's just as much the responsibility of the reserves on the sidelines to call out screens as it is ours out on the court.

When the Lakers are on the road, playing away from home, we want to communicate with each other with even more intensity than normal. We've got a lot of fans on the road, but when we go into an arena we arrive thinking that we're our only cheerleaders. We know we have to pull for one another.

The most exciting moment I can remember on the road happened when we won the championship in 1985 in Boston Garden. After we got the lead in game six, the final game of the series, I heard the greatest sound ever in that building—silence. It went from thousands of wild, crazy fans screaming for our heads to just dead quiet. We were able to win that game, and the championship, because we didn't let the noise level distract us or divide us. It was so loud at times in the Garden that we couldn't hear each other out on the floor, which was why our signals and knowledge of each other was so crucial. In the huddles we could barely hear Coach Riley, but we all knew what we wanted to do; each player knew what was expected of him. So we just went out and did it. It was probably the ultimate job of communicating that any Lakers' team has ever managed, and it won us a championship.

*The only time I can take my eyes off
Michael Jordan is when he's standing still
and we're both catching a breather.*

9

One for All

*I*t sounds like an old tune, but I've been very, very fortunate during my years in basketball. I admit it, and I think about it every time I hear other players talk about some of the basketball setbacks and troubles they had during their lives.

Michael Jordan always talks about being cut from the high school varsity team when he was a sophomore. Larry Bird has told me about the hard times he had after transferring from Indiana to Indiana State. For at least a year after he left Indiana, he wondered if he would even go back to college or remain in his hometown of French Lick. During that time, he worked as a garbageman. He said that he would've been happy to stay in French Lick and work at any job and that he had to be talked into going to Indiana State by the school's coach and his friends. It's hard to imagine what basketball would've been like for me if Bird had stayed home. A lot of things would be different. Maybe I would've had a different career completely because I wouldn't have had Bird out there motivating me to be a better player every year.

No matter what would've happened, without me and Larry being a pain in each other's side for more than ten years, life wouldn't have been nearly as much fun or as much of a challenge as it's been for both of us.

I don't have any stories about hard times in basketball. I've never been cut from a team, I've never played on a losing team—although my high school team didn't win the state championship until I was a senior—and I've always been a starter. I've also gone way beyond the goals I set out for myself in high school.

Back then, I would've been happy just to play college basketball, get my degree, and come back to East Lansing and get a job at the auto plant. All I wanted was to be able to earn enough money for an apartment and a car. That was it. If I'd attained those things out of basketball, I would have considered myself a success.

Having those goals helped me keep my perspective and made me appreciate all my teammates along the way. Sometimes, when I think about all the guys I've played with over the years who aren't playing anymore, I just shake my head in amazement. So many players have come and gone, some having had a little success in the pros and college and some none at all. That's why when kids come to my camps over the summer, one of the first things I tell them is that all of them can't become the stars of their teams, the leading scorers, the most popular players on the team, or the ones who get all the attention and publicity. The glory comes to a select group of players, a lucky few who are blessed with the talent and the dedication to develop their talents. When you consider all the junior high and high school basketball teams in the country, only five players from every team will go out for the opening tap in the games; and only one, maybe two, of those players will be the so-called stars. Even fewer of those players will go on to succeed at the college level, and even fewer of *those* players will ever reach the pros. That doesn't mean the other starters and the guys on the benches of those junior high and high school teams are any less important to the *team* than the stars. There are a lot of different ways those players can help: setting solid screens for the best shooters, grabbing rebounds, and making the quick outlet pass to start the fast break. Also important is playing tough, smart team defense, guarding the other team's best player without worrying about personal scoring goals, or simply knowing every play and option so that the player will always be in the right place at the right time and ready to make the right play. That's called playing a role, and it's probably the most important ingredient for having a successful team.

There was one time in my career when I almost forgot about the team concept. Going into my senior year at East Lansing High School, I became a very different player than the one who had played point guard for the Vikings for two years. Part of it was because I became more focused that season because of the sudden death during the summer of one of my best friends, and a teammate, Reggie Chastine. He was killed in an automobile accident that shocked our entire school, and really caused me to dedicate the next season to him. But also, I think I was affected by all of the hype that started before the season concerning where I would go to school and by being named to so many all-America teams. Suddenly, it was like I started to believe what everyone was saying, and started thinking that I could play the game by myself. I was 6'–7" then, still a lot bigger than most guards and I took advantage of that fact. It didn't hurt that the dunk rule was reinstated that summer, allowing us to dunk for the first time in years. Combine all of those factors and it's easy to see why I went basketball crazy. I averaged about 40 points per game for the first couple of weeks of the season. It was just me and the basketball.

Finally, Coach Fox called me in and laid down the rules. He told me flat out that we weren't going to win the state championship if I continued to play so selfishly. He said everybody was watching me—the fans, the opponents, even my teammates out on the floor. He said I had to start getting my teammates involved, that it was a team game, not a Magic Game. That woke me up. My next game I had 12 points and 18 assists, but more importantly, the team went on a roll. We started beating teams by an average of almost 40 points!

It was a good thing I learned to involve my teammates because we wouldn't have won the state championship that year without them. Against Brother Rice High in the championship game, I fouled out with 1:08 left on the clock and our team nursing a five-point lead. I had scored 34 points, grabbed 14 rebounds and made four assists, but they wouldn't have been worth anything if the team had lost the game. But the guys were great. They did everything they had to do down the stretch and we became state champions.

I can't put into words how important my teammates on the Lakers have been to me. I don't care how much talent we've had with Kareem, James Worthy, Jamaal Wilkes, Norm Nixon, Bob McAdoo, Byron Scott, Michael Cooper, Maurice Lucas, Mychal Thompson, and all the other players who've been so important to the team; we didn't win championships without the right chemistry, strong communication between the players and

My teammate Kareem Abdul-Jabbar, the
captain—one of the greatest players of all
time. We'll miss him.

coaches, and—despite the problems every team has to survive—a sincere respect for one another.

If the team couldn't work together, if we didn't *want* to win so badly that we put the team before personal goals and petty problems, or if we just didn't know how to win, we would not have succeeded. Not once.

The Lakers have won championships when other teams were supposed to have more talent than we did. When we beat Philadelphia for the championship in 1980 and 1982, their bench was supposed to be stronger than ours. Their coach, Billy Cunningham, played ten guys, while we were known as the "Great Eight" because Pat only went three players deep into our bench. But those eight guys played well together, and the other four were important to us in other ways. Primarily, they practiced strong against us; then during games, they supported us without complaining about not getting any playing time. Unfortunately, we didn't have that kind of harmony every season; most teams don't, and some never find it.

Our egos kept the Lakers from winning the championship twice during my first seven seasons, in 1981 and 1986, two years when we were defending champions. Of all the factors, including injuries, that kept champions from defending their titles for nearly twenty years until the Lakers won back-to-back championships in 1987 and 1988, a change in attitude is probably the most harmful. Some champions can't deal with the expectations that follow them during the next season. Other teams simply forget about the little things that made them champions in the first place, especially the way every player did his job without worrying about who was being paid the most money or getting the most attention from the media or the largest endorsement contracts.

After we won the 1980 title, the Lakers just didn't know how to be champions. Different players started thinking about themselves instead of the *team*. We'd hear guys whispering things such as "I think I should get more shots" or "I'm not getting enough playing time." Things like that became our downfall.

Complacency can also beat champions. That's what we learned five years later when we lost to the Houston Rockets in the Western conference finals in 1986 when Ralph Sampson made a miracle shot in the final seconds that eliminated us in five games. We were stunned. After the shot bounced in, Coop just

Byron Scott, my outstanding backcourt part-
ner, playing strong defense with eyes on his
man, Cleveland's Mark Price, legs spread,
knees bent.

lay on the floor underneath the basket and stared at the ceiling. He couldn't believe what had happened; none of us could. Looking back, I know now that the Rockets were the better team at that time, but I also know that as defending champions we had become comfortable with ourselves. Too comfortable. We'd beaten Houston four out of five times during the season, and we walked into the series against them thinking "Yeah, we're the Lakers."

Well, the Rockets were just rolling over everybody at that time, and they just rolled over us, too, all because we brought the wrong attitude into the series. It took all those years, but I think we finallly learned one of basketball's simplest lessons after that painful series.

At every level, coaches should outline what they expect from each of their players—from the stars to the guys at the end of the bench. In Los Angeles, Pat Riley made that responsibility one of his personal causes by developing a ratings system for the players. The system is divided into categories such as rebounding, shooting, and passing. Riley has two main concerns, whether the players perform efficiently and whether they're giving a consistent effort every night. The coaches set goal levels in every category for each player. Then after every game, they watch the tapes and assign each player a one-to-ten rating in each category—like getting grades in school.

Sometimes players don't want to hear Pat's criticisms, but the numbers don't lie. The stats are also very useful because they allow the player to see exactly which part of his game is suffering. If I'm in, say, a shooting slump, it might be affecting another part of my game. It might affect how hard I play defense, or I might be slacking off on my rebounding responsibilities. Coaches usually see these things before the players do. We can be really stubborn when it comes to how we're playing; but we can't hide from the numbers. The ratings help both the coaches and player understand quicker what's wrong than what we might be able to do on our own; so, we've learned to live with the ratings and even welcome them when we're struggling.

When everyone on the Lakers is playing well and fulfilling their personal responsibilities, we know that even the guys who play what outsiders might think are lesser roles will also gain recognition for their contributions.

Years ago in Los Angeles, all our fans realized that Kurt Rambis's role was as important to the Lakers' championships as mine, Kareem's, or James Worthy's role, even though Kurt wasn't a big

My former teammate Kurt Rambis, one of the most underrated players in the league (although not in L.A.), waits for a rebound under the boards, a familiar place for him.

scorer. Kurt was one of our tough guys. He's 6'–8'' and 215 pounds, and he played power forward for us for seven years before joining the expansion Charlotte Hornets in 1988–1989. In that time, he never averaged more than 7.5 points a game. But scoring wasn't Kurt's primary role. His role was to be intense, to rebound, and to play defense as if there was no tomorrow! Kurt did all those things for us and was recognized around the city as an important member of our team, which he was.

Kurt took a lot of pressure away from Kareem and James with his aggressiveness, his rebounding and his effort. He was usually the focal point for the other team's big man; and when somebody tried to rough up either James, Kareem, Jamaal, or myself, Kurt was right in their faces protecting his teammates. He also hustled as much as anybody. Make that *more* than anybody; so he was also one of our best offensive rebounders. And when I was running the fast break, I always kept an eye out for Kurt because I knew he'd be hustling down the floor. I also knew he had good hands; he could catch almost anything and score. That was his reward for all the hard work. He was also one of the most popular players on the team. He even had a fan club made up of some local teenagers who called themselves "The Rambis Youth" and walked around the Forum wearing black-rimmed athletic glasses like Kurt used to wear during games.

On some nights Kurt would even become the hero by scoring the big basket or making the game's big defensive play. During the finals in 1984, he became the focal point of the whole series against Boston when he was collared by Kevin McHale while driving toward the basket on a fast break in game three at the Forum. It had already been a physical, frustrating series for us, and that was the last straw. Kurt was probably the toughest guy on the team, and he bounced up from the floor ready to fight with Kevin. So did the rest of our players. We were ready to defend him at any cost because he had done it for us so many times. Unfortunately for us, we weren't ready to handle that kind of challenge.

Back then the Lakers had a reputation for being "soft" because of our fast break–playing style, and the Celtics tried to take us out of what we do best by being physical with us. This time, it worked.

Of all the players, Kurt was probably the only one who wasn't affected. When he signed with the Hornets, we were really sorry to see him go because he took so much pride in his supporting role and gave it his best effort every night. All the guys on the team were always happy for Kurt whenever he received a rousing ovation. He wasn't the Lakers' star, but he got a championship ring just like everybody else. When the Hornets made their only appearance in Los Angeles in 1988–1989, everyone in the arena stood and cheered as we presented him with the championship ring he hadn't received because he wasn't with us for the official ceremony at the start of the season. It was an emotional moment for him and a fun moment for all of us.

Of course, the importance of playing your role extends all the way down to the last player on the bench, the guy who hardly ever gets out of his warm-ups. The average fan usually forgets about that player, and the home crowds treat him like a human victory cigar.

In 1985 Chuck Nevitt was that guy for the Lakers. He was 7' 5", but he hardly played; so when he got into the game, our fans at the Forum *just knew* it was over. They cheered for him and chanted Chuck's name when we were winning easily. It was a friendly kind of thing, but I know Chuck wished to himself that he could have played more. I understood what the fans were thinking when it came to Chuck, but it wasn't exactly fair to the player. His role was significant in several ways, and how he played that role was an example for every player at any level of the game who doesn't receive much playing time. Chuck spent most of his time on the bench, but he never pouted. To him, being on an NBA team was an honor in itself. So rather than being upset about spending all his time on the bench, he used it to help the team. He and the rest of the reserves were our most vocal supporters, especially when the team was on the road. In times like these, they were the only inspiration for the players on the floor, and they helped us from getting affected by the hostile crowds.

Some nights I'd miss three or four shots in a row and start to feel pretty discouraged, but then I'd hear this voice—for two seasons, 1987 and 1988, it was towel-waving Wes Matthews—coming from our bench, saying, "Hey, just make the next one." He was always the most vocal, the most encouraging, but no matter who it was, it really helped.

On the Lakers and most other successful teams, the reserves know the most important rule to their survival: treat the practices as games. That's not only when they can impress the coaches and make their case for more playing time, but it's also the time when their contributions to the success of the team are most crucial. When Michael Cooper and I go at each other during practices, it's as if it's war and our championship rings are on the line.

Like everyone else, I have days when I don't feel like practicing. During the season, my whole body aches, and there are times when I don't want to get out of bed, let alone run around the basketball court for a couple of grueling hours. But Coop makes sure I don't feel that way for long. He pushes, grabs, and elbows me, anything he would do to an opponent during the game—and then some. Because we don't have refs at practice, the players bang each other around pretty good, too good sometimes. In games it doesn't matter who's guarding me because I've already had one of the best defensive players in the game hounding me every day during practice; nothing a defender can do will be tougher to handle than what Coop's already thrown at me. Coop knows all the defensive secrets, and he doesn't hold back. To him that's what practice is all about—helping the team any way he can.

Sometimes the reserves' role will expand beyond the norm. On the Lakers, all our players have played key roles in some of our victories. That's part of the thrill of a basketball game. No one knows who the hero will be when the final buzzer sounds. It may be the guy who came in and grabbed just 2 rebounds, but they were the 2 biggest rebounds of the game because one was an offensive rebound that gave the team an extra possession at a crucial time, while the other came off the defensive glass and helped save a close victory in the final seconds. Or maybe it was the player who set the pick for a teammate who hit the game-winning shot. The average fan in the stands may not have noticed, but every guy on the team did. To them he was one of the heroes of the game. For one night, those two guys made the difference.

The Lakers are a very close team, which can be unusual. We often socialize together at different functions around Los Angeles and it's never unpleasant. Most successful NBA teams are like that. Having that camaraderie away from the game makes it easier to cope with some of the pressures every team has to deal with on the floor, in the locker room, and on the road. Everybody on the team doesn't *have* to be best friends; but when the ball goes

James Worthy, like all my teammates, is like family.

up, everybody on the Lakers is my brother. We try to leave all problems in the locker room.

We also aren't shy about thanking each other on the court. That might seem like a minor thing; but when a player knows you appreciated that extra pass he made, that offensive rebound he worked so hard to get, or that screen he set to get somebody open he'll be glad to do it again.

During my camps, I force kids to acknowledge any teammate who gives them the ball, sets the pick, or otherwise makes the play that allows them to score. "Good pass!" or "Good pick!" is all you need to say. Sometimes a simple nod of the head will be enough to let a teammate know that you appreciated what *he* did to make the play work.

There are lots of examples in the NBA of guys who are great *team* players, players who'll do whatever it takes for the success of the team. Almost all of them play for successful teams, but some are with teams that struggle, too. It's much more difficult to be a team player when your team loses on a regular basis. Players and coaches want to point fingers at each other, but it never helps. On these teams, the true *team* player won't get caught up in trying to blame someone else. He'll accept his share of the responsibility, while still working as hard as he can every night.

I really admire someone like Buck Williams. His former team, the Nets, struggled during most of his career. They had a lot of bad luck at all levels of the organization—from management to coaching to the players—which kept them from developing a consistent strategy or becoming consistent winners. But through all the problems, it seems as if all Buck cared about was giving his team a chance to win. As a power forward, he did the team's dirty work on the boards, in the lane, everywhere. He's always been one of the league's best rebounders. The Nets didn't call many offensive plays for him; he knew he'd have to get his points off the offensive boards or in transition, and that made him even stronger on the boards. He came to work *every* night, another one of those "lunch-pail" guys. When the Lakers played the Nets, we definitely knew when Buck was on the floor, and we could appreciate the effort he made, even in terrible circumstances. During the off-season, Buck was traded to the Portland Trail Blazers, which means we'll have to face him six times a year now, rather than just two. That'll be another real challenge for A. C. Green. I know he's up to it, but quite frankly, I can't wait to see who wins.

Thurl Bailey of Utah is another team player who comes to mind. He comes off the bench for the Jazz and could start for most teams in the league, no question. But he doesn't cry about not starting. He just makes the best of the situation and does his job. He knows he's a major part of the team's success, and so does everyone in the league.

The best bench player I've ever been associated with was Wes Matthews, who was with us for both of our championships in 1987 and 1988. He was always excited about being on the team, even though he backed me up as the point guard and didn't always get to play a lot of minutes. In fact, he knew most times that he wasn't even going to play unless the score got lopsided either way. But he didn't care. He was always there to support me, or anyone. He practiced hard against me and he cheered me on during games. Every time I looked up, Wes was over there on the sidelines going crazy. If we won the game or made a tough shot down the stretch, Wes was up waving a towel and cheering as if he was the biggest fan in the world. He was just happy to be a part of it all, being one of the twelve guys. I always appreciated that.

The most common pitfall some reserves fall into is becoming satisfied with their skills. When I was in high school, some of my teammates were just happy to make the team. They wanted more playing time, but they didn't do anything to earn it. They didn't work at trying to become better players. They didn't always use their time before and after practice to their advantage by adding different skills to their game. By the next year, those guys were usually gone.

That happened both at Michigan State and with the Lakers. No matter where I've played, there were always one or two guys who just stopped trying to improve. They became complacent, then kicked back and enjoyed the show. Pretty soon, they were gone, too. For me, knowing that my father worked so hard every day, I just couldn't be complacent about basketball. He encouraged me, taught me, and spent his free time working with me; the least I could do was practice and play hard. There was always some area of my game on which I could improve. I still believe that, even as I approach the last few years of my career.

So, practices are for the players to work together, but before and after is the time when individuals try to improve their

Some of our rare relaxing moments are the ones I'll cherish most.

strengths and erase their weaknesses. After a Lakers' practice, you might see any one of twelve guys working out either by themselves, in pairs, or with one of the coaches. At the NBA level, that kind of extra effort isn't usually required by the coaches, but it's expected. It's also necessary if the player hopes to enjoy a long and productive career.

A lot of players fall into the trap of thinking "Well, this is the best I can do." They think that just because they enjoyed one good performance, even one good season, that they can stop trying to improve; so, they get lazy. Actually, it's easier to work on your strengths. It's no problem for an all-star shooter to stay out all night on the playground or in the gym and rain jumpers from the sky. It's much harder for that player to run rebounding drills by himself or work on his conditioning to become quicker on defense. But at some point, every player has to sit down and evaluate himself. He has to ask "What can I do to become a better player?" Then, he has to go for that extra skill even if the task is awkward, difficult and frustrating at the beginning. Any player, no matter what level, who thinks he's reached the peak of his skills is fooling himself. While he's loafing, someone else is down in the gym or on the playground trying to catch up or pass him. On the Lakers, we always tell each other that a little more time in the gym one day will pay off the next.

Many people believe that the athletes of today are better than the ones of the past. They see how much bigger, stronger, and quicker we are and just assume that those things also make us better. I don't necessarily agree. I think players, in general, used to be more well-rounded. Guys who were great scorers—like Oscar Robertson, Rick Barry, Walt Frazier and Pete Maravich— could also pass, rebound, and play defense with almost anybody. Look up the numbers for players like the Big O, Bill Bradley, Jerry West, and Dave Bing. They did a little bit of everything.

Bing may have been known for his jump shot, but you'd better believe he played some defense when he had to. Of course, the highlight films never show that stuff, but if you were a kid growing up anywhere near Detroit when Dave Bing played, you knew about it.

For a while at the pro level after I came into the league, there seemed to be a lot more specialization. Players were either a point guard or a shooting guard, a small forward or a power forward. If you were a center, you played center, and that was it.

Worthy uses his smooth moves and superior quickness to explode to the basket past the Celtics' Kevin McHale.

But somewhere, guys started to change and become more versatile.

Now all the best point guards, players like Mark Price, Kevin Johnson, John Stockton, and Mark Jackson, can also shoot the ball so well that you have to guard them as shooters as well as play makers. Power forwards like Karl Malone, Charles Barkley, Tom Chambers, and my teammate A. C. Green can handle the ball so well that they can drive right around you, and they can hit the open shot from long range. And centers now are becoming so multi-talented that you don't look twice anymore when a guy like Brad Daugherty of Cleveland is helping his team bring the ball up the court like a guard.

I'd like to think I had something to do with these changes. Because I was so tall, everybody thought I shouldn't be playing point guard. I had the body of a power forward, and that's where they thought I should be playing. Fortunately, I had coaches at every level who didn't think that way. They let me handle the ball so that I could do everything possible to help the team win. Now, almost every team has guards that are at least 6'–6'' or 7'', and coaches are getting less caught up in making you play one position *all* the time. Pat Riley used to say that his ideal team would be made up of five 6'–9'' guys. Well, we just might have it next season when we use a lineup of 6'–9'' James Worthy, 6'–10'' Mychal Thompson, and 6'–9'' A. C. Green in the frontcourt, and 6'–7'' Coop or 6'–4'' Byron Scott and myself at guard. With that group, teams never know which way we're going to set up, especially because James, Coop, and I are interchangeable on a lot of our plays. Who knows? Maybe that's the future of the game.

*These guys don't know which way I'm going
to go, and that's just the way I like it.*

10

Sleight of Hand

I have the nickname Magic, but every player in the NBA is a Magician. To play the game and play it well, we all need a few tricks, a bit of basketball sleight of hand. We need to know how to make our opponents think we're going to do one thing when we're really going to do something else. We've got to divert their attention from one area of the court to another, then pull a rabbit out of our hats. Or maybe we just have to use the rules to our full advantage, even if it means testing the rules. But only sometimes.

Maybe it's trickery; I believe it's something else. When I was a child learning the game from my father, another important lesson he stressed was that I learn how to *think* the game, how to *feel* the game. He taught me that the best skill I could have wasn't just being a great passer, a great shooter, a great rebounder, or even a great defensive player. He said the best skill I could have was a basketball mind.

A lot of young players overlook that skill because they think that if they can jump higher, dribble the ball faster, or outmuscle everybody then they'll become a great player. They forget about the thinking part of the game. They forget about playing smart basketball. But that's the real challenge.

As my dad and I sat in our den and watched the Pistons' games on television, I always wanted to figure out the different shortcuts that players tried to use to make the game easier, the tricks of the trade. But Dad told me not to even think about trying to take shortcuts. He said that great basketball players were knowledgeable about the game and that they had the dedication to work on their skills whenever they had the chance. He said that in basketball there were no shortcuts. He was right.

Still, everybody always wants to talk about the little tricks we use in the NBA. My campers want me to tell them about my trade secrets—how I'd trick a defender into going for a head fake or how I'd trick an opponent into fouling me while we're both going for a rebound. Then they'd tell me about some of the things they've tried to do on their playgrounds at home because they thought they saw an NBA player doing it on television or at a game.

Now, I won't lie to you. Almost every pro has a personal bag of tricks that helps him recover from certain disadvantages. Most of the tricks are just good basketball, but a lot of them are also close to cheating.

A player might try anything until he gets caught by the officials. If someone gets caught out of position under the boards when everybody's going for the rebound, he might be holding an opponent's shorts on the side as the player tries to jump. That throws the rebounder's timing off just enough for maybe one of his teammates to sneak inside for the basketball. Or maybe the player caught out of position will step on the back of the opponent's shoe. That works sometimes, too. The trouble is that those kinds of tricks hardly do the job. Refs are always on the lookout for them, and their work became easier once the league started using three officials again in the 1988–89 season. That season the game changed a lot. A lot of the action that used to happen away from the side of the floor where the basketball was—a side that was blind to two officials—stopped almost completely. It took most of the players some time to adjust to having another pair of eyes on the floor. At first, everybody was frustrated because more fouls were called, which slowed the game. But in the end, everybody's fear that pro basketball would become a free throw shooting contest didn't happen. The extra pair of eyes kept things in check and didn't leave a lot of room for tricks of the trade, even though some players still tried.

Players like Bill Laimbeer of Detroit will scream bloody murder if somebody so much as touches him when he's shooting or going for a rebound. Things like that have upset a lot of other players who feel as if they've been cheated when that kind of prize-winning performance works.

Or take the guys who make a lot of trips to the free throw line, players like Moses Malone, Bernard King, and Adrian Dantley. They've learned how to take advantage of even the tiniest bit of body contact by a defender. They use dozens of twists and fakes to make the defender do what he doesn't want to do, such as jumping in the air too soon trying to block the shot or reaching in and committing a foul. Once their defender is out of control, they'll get themselves in position where the guy will foul them while they're in the process of shooting. Finally, they'll give their shots a little extra *umph,* maybe a grunt or a yell that makes it look as if they've been hit by the defender. Truthfully, it's smart basketball, even though those things hardly ever work for most players. It's also trickery. And for players like Malone, King, and Dantley, it's a nightly ritual.

Now, I'm not saying I've never used any of the tricks when I needed to. Everybody gets into situations during games where he has to use whatever moves he has in order to make the play. The most obvious ploy I might use once in a game comes when I'm blocked out from the rebound. I'll give the player in front of me a gentle shove in the middle of the back as he goes up for the ball. If pushed too hard, the guy will fly forward. That's not the usual direction a guy goes when he's trying to jump straight up, so the referee almost always blows the whistle when he sees a player flying out of bounds right after he's left his feet. But if I give the player in front of me just enough of a push, it just looks like he mistimed his jump, and there won't be a whistle.

On the other side, just as some players know how to act as if they've been fouled when they're shooting, some of the smartest rebounders have learned to act as if they've been pushed in the back when they find that they've either mistimed their jump or are in the wrong position for the rebound. If they find themselves suddenly off-balance and see that they're not going to have a chance to grab the basketball, they'll yell, scream, and throw their arms back as if they've been hit by a hurricane. It's the oldest trick in the book.

There are some guys in this league who are better actors than players. Around the league, they talk about the "Laimbeer Flop." It's what Laimbeer does when he throws his arms and body around just to make it look as if he's been fouled. He does it anytime he's caught out of position under the boards or anytime the player he's defending drives for a shot against him.

I sometimes "act" as if I'm fouled, which many players in the league do, to try to draw a call from the referee.

Fortunately for the rest of us, the refs are getting hip to him, and we don't see him getting the calls as much as he used to. But don't think he'll stop trying.

There are some general techniques we use in the NBA that help us in certain situations. But as I've said, we don't usually get away with them on a regular basis. We'll get called for a foul, and that only gets us on the bench. But sometimes, such as in the final seconds with the game on the line, everybody gets just a little bit desperate.

A player is defending the player with the basketball, and he wants to keep that player from getting a good shot. Or he's underneath the boards willing to do anything to get the key rebound that might preserve the lead. In those cases, the defender wants to give himself every chance to stop the offensive player from making the shot, and the rebounder will want to do everything he can to get an edge against his opponent; maybe that'll include one little trick. Or two.

Even some of the best one-on-one defenders in the NBA, such as Sidney Moncrief, Michael Jordan, Dennis Johnson, and even Coop, will try this one against some of the best shooters: They'll tap a player's elbow when he's trying to shoot. That will throw the shooter's timing off just a tiny bit or, at least, distract his concentration, which can be just as effective as blocking the shot. If the defender is quick enough and sneaky about what he's doing, the refs won't see the move because most of the time they're looking for contact near the ball, such as when a defender hits the shooter's arm or wrist when he's trying to block the shot.

Norm Nixon, one of my former teammates, was one of the best in the league at that trick. In 1982 when he faced the Philadelphia 76ers in the finals, Norm was matched against Maurice Cheeks, one of the deadliest point guards in the league. Cheeks does things quietly but as well as anyone. That year, he shot 52 percent from the floor. That's high for guards because we're usually shooting from the outside, whereas forwards and centers are almost always close to the basket. Cheeks was also third in the league in assists and second in steals; so it was no secret that if we were going to beat the 76ers we were going to have to somehow shut down Maurice Cheeks.

Well, by the sixth game of the series, Cheeks was clearly frustrated, mostly because Norm had perfected the "elbow"

Ralph Sampson, then of the Houston Rockets, grabs my shirt, a little extra defense to prevent me from making the shot. Where's the ref?

technique and harassed Maurice into shooting much worse than he did in the regular season. Going into game six, we led three games to two and needed to win if we didn't want to go back and play the deciding game in Philadelphia where we'd lost games two and five.

We took an early lead and had a 9-point margin at half-time. The 76ers were getting points from their two main scorers, Julius Erving and Andrew Toney, which was the case in every game. That's why Norm's work against Maurice Cheeks was so big for us. Everything started with Cheeks; as long as Norm made him struggle, we had a chance. All during the series, Cheeks complained about what Norm was doing. Like any pro, Norm denied everything, but the smile on his face said he knew exactly what he was doing.

In the fourth game of the series, Cheeks missed ten of his fifteen shots and tried to convince everyone that Norm was fouling him every time he shot. It didn't work. In that last game, Cheeks did almost everything right. Despite our defensive pressure, he committed only one turnover, which is amazing when you're playing under the gun for the championship. Me? I had six turnovers in that game, something I'm not particularly proud of.

But what helped us most was that Cheeks missed thirteen of his nineteen shots. Norm was called for four fouls in the game, but he didn't foul out. Maurice was really frustrated, but there was nothing he could do—except get revenge.

He and the 76ers did just that the next season when they whipped us in four straight games in the finals. Their final play-off record was 12–1, the best record in NBA play-off history. The difference was that the 76ers had gotten Moses Malone, who was still in his prime and dominating the middle like Akeem Olajuwon and Patrick Ewing are today. That 1983 76ers team was probably the best team we ever faced in the finals, and that includes the 1989 Pistons. The next season, they were upset by the Nets in the first round of the play-offs, which was a bad break for them but a lucky break for everyone else because they might have won the whole thing again.

On the whole, most players try to stay away from using tricks on the court as much as possible. Tricks usually mean a guy is trying to make up for bad habits. Or maybe he wants to take the shortcuts that my father said didn't exist. There are *smarter* ways of playing the game. In the NBA, being smart is all

I use my height advantage to see over the outstretched arms of defenders like the San Antonio Spurs' Johnny Moore.

part of being able to survive. We've added subtle points to our skills because everybody does, and you've got no choice but to learn to be a smarter player or to get burned by someone who is smarter. But if you play the game straight and rely on only the most fundamental aspects of it, you're still ahead of most of your opponents.

For instance, when I have the basketball, the defensive player guarding me is looking for any sign that might give away what I'm about to do. Some guys watch my eyes; others look at my shoulders and chest. If I need to get around him and I don't think I can do it by just dribbling around or shooting over him, I'll give him something to think about: the fake. I'll use any part of my body to shake my defender—my head, shoulders, eyes, hands, and feet. If I haven't started dribbling yet, the head-and-shoulder fake is most effective, especially if I've already hit a few shots.

Another former teammate, Maurice Lucas, had the head fake down to an art. He'd hold the ball with both hands as if he was about to shoot, gaze at the rim, then make a quick motion as if he was about to launch it. The defender would almost always go for it, and Luke would either bring the ball down and drive around the guy, who was still in midair, or just let the guy land on top of him for a foul.

Larry Bird probably has the best head fake in the league. He can fake you while he's standing still or on the run. And because he's such a dangerous passer, he can fake a pass that will get his defender off-balance for just an instant, which is enough time for Larry to become open for a shot.

With a pass fake, I can get my defender to start leaning in one direction, which gives me just enough of an opening to either allow me to dribble around him, throw the real pass I want to make, or even take the shot. If I've made up my mind that I want to go left, I'll fake to the right and see what the defender does. And I don't just give it a soft fake, either. Most NBA defenders are smart enough not to go for that, especially from people like me, guys who like to pass the basketball. I have to fake hard, as if I'm really going to make the pass. So I fake with as much momentum as I can use and still have enough control to go the other way if I want to.

Sometimes it might take two or three fakes to get the defender out of position. And some guys are just too smart and quick to be faked out.

It's not "out" on me!

I don't try to force the play, which might result in taking a bad shot or making a bad pass. Fakes don't always have to work immediately. Sometimes after I've faked left for two or three possessions, the defender will think that every time I go left it's a fake. So what do I do? I go left, naturally, and leave the guy standing there wondering what happened.

Fakes can help in other situations, too. Underneath the offensive boards, I can sometimes fake the defender who's trying to block me out by moving to one spot; then when he tries to plant himself in front of me, I cut hard behind him, usually spinning in the other direction. If I'm lucky, the ball will rebound toward me, and I can tip it in. I also use fakes when I'm moving without the ball, maneuvering around and behind screens from your teammates.

One play the Lakers use is a double screen on one side of the lane, usually set by the center and power forward. While Byron Scott cuts back and forth behind it on the baseline, I'm out near the top of the key waiting for Byron to get free in the corner or in the lane so that I can get him the ball for an open shot. It's Byron's option to cut in either direction from behind the screen. Either way, I try to get the ball to him before the defender, who's stuck in the middle of the two screens, has figured out where he's gone.

Early in my career, I ran the same play with Jamaal Wilkes. He and I had true connection on the floor. I could tell where he was going almost every time. There isn't any time for signals on this play. The two guards just have to read each other and hope that they're on the same page.

When it worked as it did with Jamaal and me, the defender didn't have a chance because we read each other so well that I could almost start my pass before he'd made his cut.

It took Byron and me a few years to get to that point. He's like Jamaal in that he's just as deadly with the jump shot from the corner as he is with the lay-up or dunk. It was a matter of us learning how to read each other's eyes on the play.

To make it work, Byron usually fakes into the corner or inside—his little trick—which usually gives him just enough time to break away from his defender and gives me just enough of an opening to make the quick pass around my defender and watch the ball sail through the net. A trick of the trade? Maybe. But to me, and to my father, it's just smart basketball.

What?!!? Are you kidding me?

11

Who, Me?

Everyone in the NBA believes that they're the perfect basketball player, including me. We believe every shot we take is a good one, every pass is an assist, every defensive play is a smart one, and every move is within the rules. Unfortunately, none of us is perfect. That's why the league has officials—the traffic cops, watch dogs, and den mothers of the game, all rolled into one.

By nature, players grow to dread the officials. They're like the parents who always scold you. I never hear a word from Dick Bavetta, Hugh Hollins, Jack Madden, Darrell Garretson, Bill Oates, Ed Rush, or any of the other NBA officials unless I've done something wrong, such as "traveling" with the basketball, committing a foul, or somehow violating the rules. *Me? Never!*

Every player thinks that way because it seems that we've known the rules of the game all our lives. Long before I reached the NBA, I knew the rules of the game, the do's and don'ts every player starts to learn the first time he picks up a basketball around the house, on the playground, or in the gym. I can't even remember when I first learned that you couldn't run more than two steps without taking a dribble, that you couldn't touch the basketball if it was on the rim or inside the cylinder, that you couldn't touch a player anywhere while he was shooting, and that you couldn't stay in the lane on offense for more than 3 seconds—simple, basic things. For me, knowing these and all the other rules came from watching the older guys playing at the

Main Street Elementary School playground before I was old enough to join them, but it really seems like I've always known.

Almost every player in the NBA grew up with the game. We played with older brothers and sisters and played for hours in the backyard, on the driveway, at the local playground, or in the school gym.

By the time I was in the fourth grade, my brother Larry and I were already spending most of our time down at Main Street. He was always Walt Frazier, while I was Wilt Chamberlain. In the winters, we'd even shovel the snow off the court in order to play. Larry's one year older than I am, so he was always anxious to beat me. The reason I learned to dribble so well was because Larry used to pressure me the entire length of the court every time I had the ball. I hated him for it then, but now I'm thankful he gave me those kinds of hard lessons.

Most of us started so early in our lives that our knowledge of the rules just came naturally. By now, all of us know what we *should* do on the basketball court, but we all make mistakes. We've all been whistled for traveling, palming the basketball, and goal tending, even though we should know better. But that's where defense, the pressure of the game, and human nature become factors in the way the game is played.

Players at every level, if they're defensive-minded at all, can force other players into doing things they know they shouldn't do and don't want to do. Most of my blunders are caused by someone on the other team playing great pressure defense against me. Others are caused when I didn't read a play correctly. After all, everyone makes mistakes. Maybe I thought one of my teammates was going to cut one way when they were really going in the other direction, so I passed the basketball to the wrong area. To win, a team has to commit fewer mistakes and fewer turnovers than its opponents. Most people would be surprised to know how many players, even in the NBA, don't know some of the little rules of the game, the ones that might cause the player to commit a turnover when there was no reason for it. And we're all guilty.

In my mind, when I commit a turnover, it takes away 2 points my team should've had, and those 2 points can cost us a victory. Every time the Lakers lose by one basket, I think back to some of the turnovers I committed in the game, especially the ones that could have been avoided if I had kept my mind on the game or if I'd been that "perfect" player that I believed I was. In the 1987–88 season, the Lakers lost only twenty games. We had the best record in the league, which helped us have the home-court advantage throughout the play-offs. We won the title that year, and we owe it to having the home-court advantage in every series. The last three play-off series that year went the full seven-game limit. My teammate Mychal Thompson said we took the "scenic route" to the championship that year, hitting every bump and pothole along the way. But because every seventh and deciding game was played in front of our friendly crowds at the Forum, we had just enough of an edge to help us win. That year, the Lakers lost six games by 1 or 2 points. I averaged just under 4 turnovers in every game, so, by my calculation, I cost my team a potential 8 points every night. The next year those mistakes were more costly. While I averaged about the same number of turnovers per game, the Lakers lost more games. Our 57–25 record was the best in the Western conference, good enough to give us the home-court advantage through the conference finals, but not as good as the Pistons who qualified for the home-court advantage during the entire play-offs by having the best record in the league, 63–19. But one thing the Lakers learned through the years was to overcome our mistakes and not become rattled by mistakes, opposing crowds, and officials. I think that showed when we stormed through the conference finals without losing once in eleven games. We reached the NBA finals against Detroit with a perfect record, the first time in league history that's ever been done. As Mychal Thompson said, "This time, we flew direct."

I don't honestly know whether or not the home court made much of a difference in the finals last year. We lost the first two games on the Pistons' floor, but without Byron and considering that I might have been hurt in the second game no matter where it was played, I don't know what our chances would have been had we had the home-court edge and played the first two games at the Forum. I think we would have at least split the first two games, no matter what happened. In front of our crowd, we would have at least had a chance. But considering the bad luck we experienced, and the way the Pistons were focused on winning the championship, we hardly had a chance. Things like that happen. We, as a team, just had to accept that we have to prepare for the next season as if we're still looking for our first championship.

If mistakes can hurt a team's chances, arguing and finger pointing among the players and disputing the officials can kill them. One of the most difficult basketball lessons for me to learn was that sometimes there's nothing I can do about committing turnovers. When a team or opponent plays good defense against me and forces me to cough up the ball or make a bad pass, all I can do is shake my head and try to make sure it doesn't happen again. When I play against guys like Dennis Johnson, Michael Jordan, Maurice Cheeks, Mark Jackson, John Stockton, and Kevin Johnson, the best point guards in the league, I *know* I'm going to make at least one mistake. They're all such smart defensive players that I can't leave the locker room expecting to have a perfect night against them. I still *try,* but what I can expect every night is that I won't make "stupid" mistakes, which I won't do if I'm playing smart basketball. Those are the turnovers that hurt me most, and the ones I think about for a long, long time.

In my camps, I always stress to the young players that they should study the rules so that they'll know what they can and can't do in different situations. I also believe it's important to respect the officials, as much as that might be difficult at times. Players always believe they're getting a raw deal from the refs. In most cases, we're wrong.

The referees try to do the best job they can to keep the games under control and up to NBA standards. Sure, they make mistakes, too, and I've been known to dispute a call every so often myself. But I don't allow my campers to argue with the officials. They have to learn that when the referee makes the call arguing about it will only get them in trouble. The player will either get charged with a technical foul or the officials will start watching him like a hawk. They'll scrutinize every move the player makes and maybe get even tougher on the player as the game progresses. I just remind them that if Michael Jordan, Larry Bird, Akeem Olajuwon, Charles Barkley, Tom Chambers, and I can make turnovers every night, how can anyone expect the refs to be perfect?

Keeping your temper over questionable calls is sometimes easier said than done, especially in the intense heat of the action, or on a particular night when you're frustrated because you think everything is going against you. That's when players get angry at themselves, the coach, their teammates, anything and everything. And the easiest person to take it out on is the ref. I've been guilty of that, too.

*When you're fighting for a championship
ring, there's no time for friendship.*

Twice in my NBA career I've been thrown out of games for arguing calls, and those were the two dumbest nights of my life. The last time came in December during the 1988–89 season when the Lakers were in the midst of the worst losing streak of my career. We had lost nine straight games on the road, which tied a record for the Lakers franchise. The talk around the league was that we were washed up. People said Kareem was too old, Coop was past his prime, Byron was inconsistent, and James Worthy just wasn't playing like he had been during his best seasons. They said I was the "only" thing the Lakers had going for them, like I was the only talented player in a Lakers' uniform. For once, we let the talk get to us.

Sure, we had our troubles, but people were wrong about the Lakers; I think we proved that in the play-offs. Weeks into the season, it was like we were already trying to adjust to life without Kareem, even though he had nearly an entire season to play before retiring. We were just having a difficult time, and it caused us to become tense and touchy about ourselves. Even though Coach Riley said before the season that Kareem would play less of a role for us, some of the players were criticizing him as I'd never seen. We were losing our confidence. Amazingly we never fell out of first place during the season, even though the Phoenix Suns chased us until the final week. But things were bad in December, really bad, and one night I just lost my head.

The team was in Phoenix for a game that was very important for both teams. The Suns were revamped during the off-season. After having been ravaged by a messy drug scandal during the 1987–88 season in which none of the players was ever proven wrong, they got rid of most of their familiar names— Walter Davis, James Edwards, and Larry Nance and brought in an entirely new cast. Now they were led by players like Tom Chambers, Eddie Johnson, and Kevin Johnson, all of whom were hungry to win. They wanted to play for a champion, and they got off to a start in the fall that surprised everybody, even us. So here we come limping into Phoenix with the Suns wanting to prove that they were going to be contenders. It wasn't any surprise that we were losing again; nothing was going our way anywhere. But then when I was called for a foul on a play I thought should have gone the other way, I went crazy. Before I knew it, the official charged me with two technicals. In the NBA, two technicals in a game results in an automatic ejection. I was standing there near the baseline, fuming, when I suddenly realized that I'd been thrown out of the game. On my way to the locker room, I felt embarrassed. All I could think about was how I had let my teammates and coaches down. We lost that game, and I vowed not to let myself get thrown out again.

I think players are always trying to control their emotions, but the game has become so much faster, and the stakes are so much higher, that it's a miracle somebody doesn't lose it almost every night. That's where the role of the officials is important. When the players and coaches are out there whining, complaining, and moaning about every little thing that goes against them, it's not a game. It's a nursery. But when tempers get out of control, it's dangerous.

Fortunately, I don't have a reputation with the officials as a guy who complains a lot, so I can question some of the calls without worrying whether the refs will retaliate or think I'm trying to embarrass them in public. I've always tried to establish some sort of rapport with the league's officials, whether it's with a friendly tap after a close call or a quick word of encouragement. I have some compassion for the job they're trying to do. But if I talk too much, I know I'll take myself out of the game because I'll lose my focus, and that's the last thing I want to happen when I'm facing Nate McMillen, Joe Dumars, or Alvin Robertson, three defensive players who love to give me fits when we face each other.

For the most part, leave the talking to the officials to the coach. I have enough things to worry about without being caught up in the officiating. Every season the league changes the rules slightly, whether it's making adjustments in the regulations against playing zone defenses or changing the restrictions on defensive players. It's the players' responsibility to learn the changes. The refs are learning all the time, too, and sometimes they've got to make decisions in the blink of an eye.

The most difficult call to make is the charging–blocking call when one player crashes into the defensive player while driving to the basket. The difference is usually whether the defensive man has established his position with both feet firmly on the ground. Well, it's almost impossible to watch the defender's feet and the offensive player, too. But a ref has to make that call dozens of times every night. And it's purely his judgment, which doesn't mean he's always right. But I haven't met a ref yet who changed his mind because a player tried to talk him out of it. Talk about wasting your breath!

A charge? A block? It's one of the toughest calls a referee has to make.

I also haven't met an official yet who deliberately blew a call. And when the refs blow it, they know it. Players and coaches don't have to tell them. Sometimes I'll let the official know I disagreed with his call, but only in a subtle way. I might whisper to him as the game is going on or maybe just give him a look that gets my point across; but that's about it.

When it comes to dealing with officials, it's perception that matters. They don't want it to look as if they're being shown up by players or coaches. That's why a player who throws up his arms in disgust might get charged with a technical foul, whereas a guy who says something under his breath might be allowed to get away with it. What matters to officials is *how* it looks. Toward the end of last season, Alvin Robertson, then playing for San Antonio, was ejected from a game when he tossed a basketball toward an official who wasn't looking and the ball hit the ref in the butt. The player said he hadn't meant to hit the official, but the ref thought he was being ridiculed. Later, the league office reviewed the tapes of the incident and found that Robertson hadn't tried to hit the official, and the fine that comes with every ejection was rescinded.

Players are usually allowed to talk to officials during the games, but we can't say just anything. As everyone knows, there are certain "magic words" that will get a player a technical foul even if he has a smile on his face. For the most part, it's best to leave a bad situation alone and leave it to the officials to try and correct it.

If it wasn't a major play, the ref might even quietly apologize. I've heard refs say, "Hey, I missed it. Sorry." If it was a critical call, I'm never surprised if the next critical call goes against the team that benefited from the last call. I'm not accusing the refs of using "make-up calls" to correct their mistakes, but it's usually pretty strange when what *seems* like a make-up call happens almost immediately after a controversial call. Usually, players or coaches don't complain because they realize what has happened and that, in the end, the calls are usually even. We just learn to live with it and go on because there's no time to whine.

My advice to my campers is to just play ball, take the calls, and then run to the other end of the court and continue playing. I tell them to be mentally tough and forget about arguing with the officials. It's not worth the fight.

There are some ways in which I try to make the officiating easier to live with for my team. For starters, I know that just as every player has his own particular playing style and tendencies, every referee has a style and tendencies in the way he calls the games. Some of the officials are more lenient on certain plays, whereas other refs, particularly newer ones, call everything strictly by the book. Also, officials adjust from game to game, team to team, player to player. That's why, for players and coaches, the early minutes of a game are a "feeling-out" period when everyone on the floor gets used to the atmosphere and the tone of the game. Players are checking out the lights, the feel of the backboards, the spring in the rims, our teammates, and our opponents. We also try to be aware of how the officials are calling the game. We try to figure if they're calling it tight, where even a gentle bump is a foul, or loose, by allowing players to be physical underneath the boards and on defense without hearing any whistles.

Everyone knows that the officials become less strict as the play-offs progress, and it's something to which we all have to adjust. Plays that would've been fouls during the regular season go unnoticed in the play-offs, which I think is good. It separates the toughest teams from the complainers. The championship is a big prize, and you've got to earn it. Officials shouldn't just give offensive players any call during the postseason, and no one wants to see a game decided by an official's call, not even the officials themselves. That's why it's important for us to adjust our games to the level of the officials, or the games will never flow into exciting, entertaining basketball.

In the regular season and the play-offs, officials usually begin the night by calling plays closely so that tempers don't get out of hand. Then they adjust as the game goes on. In the final minutes, especially when the games are close, the refs usually let the players play on no matter what happens, but only to a certain extent. Nobody wants to see 47 minutes and 50 seconds of basketball only to have the game decided at the free throw line in the final 10 seconds; that's why at the end the officials usually try to allow the outcome to be decided team against team, the way it should be.

Most players know this and they adjust their own games accordingly. Some guys are masters at playing to the exact level of the officials. They're the players, guys like Moses Malone, who hardly ever foul out. By the end of the 1988–89 season, the veteran Hawks' center hadn't fouled out of a game in more than *eleven years,* not since the 1977–78 season, which was before I

If this is a noncontact sport, then why am I down here when the ball is up there?

Even the officials have to learn to take their lumps.

even came into the league. That's incredible, especially considering all the contact the big guys create under the boards going for
rebounds and trying to score. My record for fouling out isn't so
bad. I've only fouled out five times in my career, including once
during the 1988–89 Western conference. Once again, it was my
father who taught me the importance of knowing how to read
the officials in the opening minutes of games. He told me that I
couldn't be the most valuable anything if I was sitting on the
bench.

Finally, when it comes to officials, it never hurts me to
know the names of the men who officiated in the league,
whether it was the Big Ten or the NBA. A "Good evening,
Mr. So-and-So," or "Nice call, Joe" never worked against me. Of
course, on most nights it didn't make any difference that I was
nice to the officials, but you never know when kindness and
respect might come into play when it's time to make that big
charging or blocking call down the stretch. I know refs try to be
as impartial as they can, but they're human, too. Human beings
are affected by their emotions, whether they like it or not. Never
underestimate the value of a little respect.

In 1988–89, the NBA added a third official to the crews for
the first time in eight years. For the players, that meant getting to
know a whole new group of refs. It took a while, but pretty soon
we got to know the types of calls that the different officials liked
to make. I went out of my way to try and learn the names of the
new refs. Some coaches even keep track of their team's win-loss
record with different officials.

With the new refs, it was almost like breaking in a group of
college freshmen; but they were the authority figures, so we had
to be really careful about how we treated situations. Most of the
new refs came from different college conferences, which meant
that they were seeing some things in the NBA that they hadn't
seen before. Some of the rules were different, too.

In college, teams can play any type of zone they wish; in the
NBA, there are so many restrictions that I don't think anyone in
the league really knows all the violations. Some rules, like traveling, are just called differently in the NBA than they are in college.
For the first few weeks of the season, the new refs were killing
the players on all kinds of calls, especially traveling. We'd make
the same move we've been making for years and—boom!—a
rookie ref calls traveling.

It was frustrating, but it was sometimes funny because some of the players would look for help from veteran officials after the rookie made the call. But the veterans would just shrug their shoulders and look the other way. We all had to let the rookies work through their first season because, most important, we didn't want to get started on the wrong foot with them, even if we thought that foot was traveling by mistake.

Pat Riley and I have a little "heart to heart."
Coach, I've got it under control.

12

OK, Coach

I've been fortunate throughout my career to have great relationships with almost all my coaches. From George Fox at Everett High School to Jud Heathcote at Michigan State through Jack McKinney and Pat Riley of the Lakers, I've been blessed to play for coaches who helped me improve my skills and allowed me to play the kind of up-tempo, fast-break basketball I like best. The only relationship with a coach that still haunts me is the one with Paul Westhead, who became the Lakers' coach thirteen games into my rookie season when McKinney suffered a severe head injury in a bicycle accident.

Westhead was a former college coach from LaSalle in Philadelphia who joined McKinney as assistant coach for my rookie season. He quoted Shakespeare and got along well with the players as he helped us learn the system McKinney began installing during training camp. It was a system that relied on moving the basketball up the floor as quickly as possible and allowed me to be creative within the framework of our strengths. It also allowed me to make decisions, to be in control. As I crossed midcourt, the game was full of options for me because McKinney had faith in my abilities, and there were few restrictions.

When Westhead was named head coach after McKinney's accident, he didn't change anything throughout the rest of the season because he really didn't know how to make us a better team than we were at the time. We played confidently, and the players' skills complemented each other well. Paul just let us play under the same system. We were on a roll that didn't end until we won the championship over the Philadelphia 76ers. For me, it was a storybook rookie season.

But the fairy tale didn't last long. We arrived at training camp the next fall and learned that Paul was throwing the whole system out the window. He wanted to install his own system, and nothing the players said could change his mind. Paul's system wasn't complicated, but it was strict. Every possession was designed to be run a particular way. There was no room for creativity. We ran the break, but if we didn't score right away, Paul put the breaks on hard and sent us through a series of moves that didn't take advantage of our skills. It was basketball his way, not the Lakers' way.

We tried it, but nothing worked. All the fun was gone, all the spirit that carried us to the championship the year before. We were a team that knew how it played best but couldn't, and it was frustrating for everyone. Because of our talent, we were still winning a lot of games; we thought that would be enough to get us through the play-offs. That's when we learned it takes more than talent to win championships.

In the play-offs, we were stunned by the Houston Rockets in the first-round miniseries. The Rockets won 3–2. It was even more of an insult because the two games we lost were both at home. Kareem took a lot of blame for the loss because Moses Malone was the Rockets' center and he put up some big numbers in the series. But it wasn't Kareem's fault, it was a total team breakdown, probably the worst we had during my entire career. No one did their part, including me. And we all knew it.

When we came back for my third season, Westhead tried to install the same system. Eleven games into the season, I decided I couldn't play that way, and I asked to be traded. Looking back, I realize that I didn't handle the situation very well. I made my feelings known through the media, which created a stir that went beyond anything I had intended. Before it stopped, Westhead was gone, and I looked like the bad guy. Now I know I should have kept my feelings to myself.

I didn't mean for Westhead to be fired. I guess I was naive to think I would be traded before the coach was fired, but I was honestly ready to play somewhere else.

Instead, Westhead was replaced by Pat Riley, who had been the team's color commentator alongside Chick Hearn before joining Westhead as an assistant in 1980, and General Manager

Jerry West. It took Pat a while to become comfortable with the idea of being the head coach, but once he did, Jerry returned to the front office and the Lakers went on about our business—the business of winning championships.

Coaching isn't easy and the relationship between the coach and his players is very important to the success of the team. Every coach has his own style and philosophy about how the game should be played, but sometimes he struggles to match his philosophy with the skills of his players. Most players think that their coach has to adjust to them, and that's somewhat true because the most successful coaches take their players and mold their systems around the players' talents. That's what the best coaches do, guys like Don Nelson, Lenny Wilkins, Rick Pitino, and Bernie Bickerstaff. But players have to adjust to the coaches, too. I've had coaches with different strengths, and each of them taught me something about the game that I still carry with me today.

George Fox, at Everett High School, was a guy who believed in drills, drills, and drills—in that order. That's almost all we did at practices, over and over again. Sure, we scrimmaged, but if we made too many mistakes Coach Fox wouldn't hesitate to send us right back to basics. Having a coach with that attitude helped me learn how to react quicker to changing situations in games, because, after your body repeats a specific move enough times in a drill, the move almost becomes instinctive. Those instincts allow me to react quicker than my opponent when I really need to.

On the court, in practices or games, we did what Coach Fox asked us to do or we didn't play. You've heard the term "My way or the highway?" Well, the highway ran right alongside our gym in East Lansing, and it was always waiting for every one of us, as far as Coach Fox was concerned. To him, being in the gym and playing basketball was a privilege. He thought we should treat it as a privilege by playing hard every time we walked through the door. I didn't have to think twice about believing him, not with my father at home working *two* jobs. Once when I was a sophomore, though, I came to practice one day with a bad attitude; I didn't want to be there at all. I played hard in the games, but I figured I'd use practices as my time off. I was young and felt there were other, more important things to do than practice. Practice wasn't a challenge; it was boring. So like any kid, I tried to see what I could get away with. I started slacking off a bit, giving a little bit less every day.

Well, eventually Coach Fox called me into his office. He said that if I didn't play hard in practice, it said to him that I wasn't going to play hard in the games, either. And because I wasn't going to play hard in the games, he wasn't going to start me in the next game. That woke me up. I thought I was untouchable but found out I was wrong.

From then on, I came to practice every single day ready to go all-out—at Everett, at Michigan State, and with the Lakers. Coach Fox was trying to tell me that I couldn't turn the intensity on and off between the practices and games. I had to practice as if I was going to play until it became second nature.

Now if you ever saw a Lakers' practice, you'd see twelve guys going at each other so hard you'd think they didn't like each other. Well, that's not true, of course. But to us basketball is a business, and we have to come to work every day with our lunch pails and briefcases, just like people in every line of work. The sooner I learned to have that attitude, the sooner I was on my way to becoming a serious and better player.

Don't get me wrong. Playing for Coach Fox was also fun. Playing for him taught me the benefits of hard work. We had a lot of talent on our team, but not so much talent that the coach thought we were too good to practice the fundamentals or run all the drills he thought were so important. But he always kept the practices balanced. He rewarded his players with scrimmages and more playing time, which made it easier for us to give our last ounce of energy during practices when we all would rather have been somewhere else. The players wanted to play hard for him because he recognized and cared for us as individuals, just like any father would. He was a guy we could talk to when we needed someone to listen. Having that kind of coach, someone who's more than a coach, is very important for young players.

If the coach reaches out to his players away from the floor, it shows he's not afraid to be the players' friend, as well as their coach. That's not an easy thing for most coaches to accomplish. We took full advantage of Coach Fox's concern and desire to make us better people, and it paid off for all of the players. When we saw Coach Fox away from the gym, we saw him in a different light. I have tremendous respect for the man. He was really nice, and he made me feel good about being myself. And not just as a basketball player. He was tough, but even on his worst days, those days when we ran so many suicide drills that we thought he was the meanest man in the entire world, we knew deep down inside that he truly cared for us. In high school, or at any level, that's all you can ask of a coach.

At Michigan State, Jud Heathcote made it clear what he wanted from us: perfection. When it came to running the plays, no one could deviate from what he had designed for us. We had to run the plays precisely every time, no questions asked. That taught me basketball discipline and forced me to learn the necessary patience needed to execute a play through all of its options until it works. Having that patience is especially critical for me now down the stretch in NBA games when the Lakers are behind and the pressure to score a basket is unbelievable. It's those times when I think back to the lessons of discipline Jud Heathcote taught me and give thanks.

There was no mistake about that when I moved from high school to Michigan State. With Heathcote, I knew I was moving to another level. If you didn't go to practices on time, attend study halls, and go to classes, it was over. No questions asked. He definitely had the entire program running his way. I never had major problems with Jud, even though he was one of those hollering coaches. He'd yell and scream at me about anything. If my shirt wasn't tucked in, he'd holler. If I had messed up on a drill, he'd holler. If I wasn't hustling, he'd holler. Sometimes I thought he hollered at me just to practice hollering. I learned to adjust to that, too, even though there were some days when I just didn't feel like being hollered at. Those were just bad days for everybody, but Jud could holler at any of us and get away with it because he had everybody's respect. He knew how to motivate us, to balance the moods. He'd scream at me, then the next time when I thought he was going to holler, he'd say, "Hey, it's all right." That made me try harder next time. He was also one of the best coaches, in terms of preparation, that there ever was.

When it came to scouting our next opponents, then giving us just enough to make the games easier for us, Jud was a master. Sometimes I thought we knew more about an opponent than they knew about themselves. That's why we won the NCAA championship my sophomore season; it was preparation.

As I moved on into the NBA, I was lucky enough to find myself being coached by Jack McKinney. He didn't try to make the players do things they couldn't do just for the sake of some theory. We had Kareem in the middle; he was still one of the most dangerous centers in the game, and everything revolved around him. Jamaal Wilkes played small forward. He was one of the best shooters I ever played with, probably the very best, and he had great hands. Jamaal could handle any pass I threw at him. He was also probably the very best teammate I ever had at moving without the basketball. He was so smooth moving in and around screens and then floating that nice soft jumper through the rim that we called him "Silk."

The power forward was Jim Chones, a big, strong player who, like Kurt Rambis, took a lot of pressure off Kareem. Norm Nixon and I were in the backcourt. We were both good passers; it didn't really matter who ran the offense, but because Norm had a reputation as a shooter, our roles just naturally developed: I played point guard, and Norm played shooting guard.

Jack took all our skills and developed the perfect system for us, a nice mixture of half-court screens that took advantage of our passing skills and the running game. Jack knew we could run, and he didn't mind giving us the freedom to run every chance we got. Everybody knew their respective roles; so we just played the same way every night. Naturally, the longer we all played together, the better we got, until all the plays became so natural it seemed as if we were always on the same wavelength and that's unusual.

Take the simple backdoor play I used to run with Jamaal. By midseason, it became almost unstoppable. We'd either score or they would double team Jamaal really quick, which opened up someone on the other side, the weak side, usually for a jam by either Kareem or Jim Chones.

Because of my size, Jack had me crashing the offensive boards. When I got the ball, it allowed us to start our fast-break even quicker because it eliminated the outlet pass from the re-bounder to the point guard that most teams need to start their break. I just got the ball, turned, and was gone. Pretty soon, everybody started calling our fast-break "Showtime!" The term caught on, and although teams all over the league tried to run as much as we did, nobody else had "Showtime!" except the Lakers. It happened because Jack watched every player, measured what he could do, then created a system that would fit everyone's needs. It was really a shame that he got hurt so soon into my rookie season because we were rollin', really rollin'. He was never the same as a coach after the accident, and he never really received credit for what he achieved with the Lakers. What happened to him is one of the saddest things that I've ever experienced in my career.

Riley is an excellent Xs and Os coach. Like Jud, he wants you to carry out everything exactly the way he's drawn on the blackboard, whether it's in practice or in a game. He wants you to carry out his instructions, whether it was how to play defense against a particular player or how to execute a certain strategy he believes might be the key to the game. There's nothing wrong with coaches requiring that their players be precise and disciplined, but with all the talented players in college and the pros, I believe coaches need to be flexible, too. They must understand and consider their players' skills, and mold their system in such a way that everyone receives the maximum benefit. Paul Westhead wanted the Lakers to run his system whether it was the best system for the Lakers or not; Pat Riley knows that what the Lakers do best is run with the basketball so that's what he wants us to do. In fact, he's fascinated with the fast-break. He's broken down the break to such an extent that it's almost a science to us. The moment we get the ball off the defensive glass, every player has a particular responsibility. The guy who gets the rebound, usually A. C., or James, looks for me immediately. When I get the basketball from them, I dribble to the middle of the floor; that way I can run the play to whichever side of the defense becomes open. In most cases, we have more players on offense than the opposition has on defense, so somewhere, something has to give. The defense can't cover the whole floor. The two fastest guys fill the lanes on either side of me. That's usually Byron Scott and James. James may be the best player in the league on the break. He's quick, he's smart, and once I get the ball to him, he explodes to the basket, virtually unstoppable. He's usually my first but not my only option. Besides having Byron on the other side, I have a third player, usually A. C. Green, following the play as the trailer in the middle of the floor. He first looks for a pass in what we call our "secondary" fast-break, the options that come when both James and Byron are covered. Then he looks for the offensive rebound, which is usually easier to grab during the chaos of a fast-break because the defense doesn't always have time to organize itself and block players out. With all these options, the Lakers usually score when we can run the ball, which is why so many teams try everything to slow us down. It may look like free-form basketball when the Lakers run the break, but it's really designed and constructed down to the smallest detail. To Pat fast-break basketball is like physics. That's what makes the Lakers what they are—running basketball at its best.

Pat Riley, one of the best "X and O" men in the game, diagrams a play during a time-out.

As much as Riley demands discipline, he's also a players' coach. Although he was never a star during nine years in the NBA when he played for five teams, including the Lakers, he understands the needs of all the players. Everybody knows about his designer wardrobe, slicked-back hair, and Hollywood looks. And they know that through the years he's developed into a talented coach. He's the league's all-time winningest coach in percentage (.728) for the regular season and for the play-offs (.700). And in 1988–89, he almost matched the Celtics' legendary Red Auerbach as the winningest coach in play-off history. When we won game four against Phoenix in the conference finals, it gave Pat his 98th play-off victory, one less than Auerbach. He's become a star in his own right. He even has a few endorsement contracts. He does television commercials, appears in newspaper and magazine ads, and is a spokesman for several causes. But he is still a players' coach.

He understands the players' hearts and minds. He knows when to push us and when to back off. He knows how to keep the starters from becoming jealous with each other, while keeping the last guy on the bench motivated to come to practice every day and play as hard as he can. Anytime players and coaches are around each other for extended periods, there'll be tensions; Pat knows how to diffuse those tensions. He's sensitive to the emotions of the guys who play. Because he was an NBA player, Pat experienced all the different moods that a player feels, from elation to depression to rejection. Everybody has problems, and often the coach has to deal with those problems because they can affect the success of the season. Pat knows how to sense problems and bring them out into the open before they tear us apart.

But don't get the idea that Riley is soft. He's as tough on the players as any coach I've ever played for. And there's no question that, when it comes down to the final analysis, he's the coach and we're the players. He listens to us, but he still has the final word.

Pat's also aggressive, and that's how we play. He's intense, and that's also how we play. We play aggressive on defense; then we try to do our thing with intensity on offense. We don't back down to anyone. For a long time, people thought we had more finesse than what is required by hard-nosed, physical basketball. They got caught up in the "Showtime!" image created with our fast-break style. It took years for us to beat that rap, and it

Coach Riley is never shy about getting his point across.

probably didn't happen until we beat the Celtics in Boston for the championship in 1985. After that, nobody could say we weren't as tough as any team in the league. That acknowledgement meant as much to us as winning the championship because we didn't feel we were getting respect for being a tough team. If any team wants to get physical with us, we'll get physical.

I think we showed that again in the 1988 championship series against Detroit. Playing against guys like Rick Mahorn, Bill Laimbeer, and Dennis Rodman, we were supposed to go soft, but we showed we can mix it up when you want to mix it up. When the Pistons took James Worthy down during one of the early games of the series, everybody came up wanting to fight. During the 1989 finals, the games never really passed beyond the normal physical intensity of the playoffs. The games were tough, and my teammates matched the Pistons shove for shove when they needed to. But it was hard to stay intense when the team wasn't at full strength. When it's a 4–0 sweep, only one team is doing most of the giving, while the other is simply taking. I think the Lakers forced the Pistons to give everything they had in the four games, and considering the circumstances of the series, that was as much as we could ask for.

Probably the biggest difference in the latest Lakers' teams and the team that lost to Boston in 1984 is our ability to play physical basketball. When the Celtics challenged us that year with rough tactics, we didn't know how to act. Kevin McHale clotheslined Kurt Rambis in the fourth game of the series, and we just rolled over. We lost that game and the series was tied 2–2. But because the Celtics were confident they could intimidate us, the series might as well have been over. That's why we lost in seven games. After that embarrassment, we learned from then on that when somebody challenged us we have to respond. We learned a lot from those seasons. In 1988 we challenged the Pistons, verbally and physically, and we wanted to find out if they could take it as well as they could dish it out. They could, but we won the championship that year and that was the bottom line. Now, the "real series" is even, 1–1.

Let me make this clear: I don't condone fighting, and I agree with the way the league deals with players who get involved in fights. They should be ejected from the game and fined. But the stakes have become so high in the NBA play-offs that emotions are going to erupt like volcanoes. Playing for the championship is

an honor that's worth fighting for, but it isn't a reason
for fighting.

Like my other coaches, Pat also thinks that players should be
rewarded for their efforts; so every once in a while when we arrive in the morning for practice, get taped and ready to play, Pat
will call us into a huddle at midcourt. He'll go over his issues,
usually his critique of the last game, and then he'll issue a
challenge: Each of us will take one shot from midcourt. If one of
us makes it, no practice; we all go home. Talk about motivation!
We're at the point where one of us makes it about half the time;
so when you see a Lakers' player bury a spectacular midcourt
shot at the buzzer, remember that we've been practicing.

The most difficult task for any coach is to find that delicate
balance between being a strict disciplinarian and having the
players want to do anything for him. I think they all want to be
liked as well as respected, even those who seem to approach
coaching like Marine drill sergeants who don't care whether the
players like them or not. A lot of coaches just don't know how
to gain the respect of their players. Fortunately, I've never played
for a coach like that. I respected Paul Westhead, as did the rest of
the team; I still do. I was happy for him when he started having
success at Loyola–Marymount University in Los Angeles. Ironi-
cally, the Lakers practice in the L–M gymnasium. For a long time
it was awkward because Westhead and I tried to avoid each other.
Some afternoons I would see him sitting at the top of the empty
stands during our practices, and I would flash back to everything
that happened several years ago. We just weren't the right match
at that time. Both of us were still in the early stages of our NBA
careers and simply unable to resolve our differences. To have just
one incident like that in my career is lucky.

Arguments and conflicts with coaches are inevitable, but for
the most part they're arguments that the player is going to lose.
Period. There'll always be problems on a team. Everybody can't
play all the minutes, everybody can't take all the shots, and
everybody can't be the star. When things get tense, it's easy to
blame it on the coaches. But I try to remember that the coach
is dealing with all kinds of pressures just as I am. He's trying to
win games and blend together twelve different people who aren't
always thinking the same way. I don't envy coaches at all, believe me.

At every level, from high school to the pros, coaches are just
trying to do their best to keep their jobs. But his job is more

than just winning games. He sometimes has a family to support and kids that might even be the same ages as his players. He's trying to earn a living so that his family can have food, clothes, and housing. Now that's pressure, and I don't think any coach would intentionally jeopardize his ability to take care of his family by doing something contrary to winning. Remembering that makes it easy for me to realize that the coach is simply trying to cope with basketball the best way he knows. He wants to win as much as I do, probably more. Of course, in doing what they think is right, coaches sometimes do the wrong thing when it comes to what's really best for the team. So some coaches do get fired. I've decided that it's not my job to tell the coach how to coach; it's my job to play. Every player should remember that.

Another aspect of coaching that I feel is important is the level of respect for the coach the players have to bring to the gym every day, whether it's for a practice or a game. I teach that lesson from the first day of my summer camps. Nobody ever talks back to a counselor, whether the counselor is right or wrong. The coach is still the coach, and the campers must respect the man or woman in that position if the team's going to succeed. No matter what players feel is right, they should try the strategy the coach's way first; then both sides can evaluate whether it works. No one has to tell me how hard it is to do that every day. In the heat of a difficult practice, when the players are frustrated because something isn't going right or when emotions get high during a game and the coach brings a player to the bench, it's hard for that player to think about respect. It's one of those times when the player might not like what he hears but he has to go along with it because the alternative—as I learned from Coach Fox—is not playing at all.

Of course, there will be times when the player just doesn't want to hear criticisms from the coach, especially if it's from a coach who yells a lot. Maybe the player has had a bad day, an argument with his wife, girlfriend, or parents, something like that. But he still has to go along with the coach because the gym is his domain. Anything that happened to the player outside those walls doesn't matter. So when the player is thinking about exploding at the coach, whether at practice or during a game, the smartest action for him is just to nod his head and say, "I hear you," and let it go at that. There's nothing the player can do that will make the situation better. Arguing only makes it worse.

On the other hand, a player shouldn't be afraid to approach his coach later in a mature way and talk about whatever problems there might have been. The worst thing in the world is to let little frustrations become big frustrations. Coaches know that a happy player plays better basketball, so most of them are willing to listen to their players' problems and help them the best way they can.

All these lessons are especially important for those who are the best players on their teams. They may be the big shot on the floor, but inside the lines, on the court, the coach is the boss. On the Lakers, I try to help out some of the younger players who might be getting frustrated because they're not getting a lot of playing time or maybe not getting enough shots. But the way I help them best is by example. If they were to see me throwing a tantrum, pouting, or doing something else that shows disrespect for Pat, the Lakers might as well end the season right there because I would undermine team unity, which is one of the most important strengths—or weaknesses—of any team.

Injuries are every player's greatest fear. But they're a part of the game we've all learned to live with.

13

Stayin'
in the Game

When my campers arrive for their week of
basketball with me during the summer, I try to start on the right
foot in terms of understanding the importance of conditioning,
proper stretching, and nutrition. So at the beginning of the week
I get everybody into the gym and tell them to take a deep breath
and to take a few laps as fast as they can. Everybody's fresh and
eager, and they don't get too winded until about the seventh or
eighth lap. Then I tell them to run around the floor a few more
times, and all smiles are gone. Then I'll say, "OK, everybody, let's
do twenty push-ups, about a hundred jumping jacks, and run
around the room some more." Now I'm the least favorite man in
the entire world. When they finish all that, I tell everybody that
we're going to play one on one, full court. Every year, somebody
says, "Come on, sir. No way! We're tired." That's when I go into
my speech about conditioning.

"Too tired? Too tired to run to the other end of the floor
and play defense? Too tired to grab the rebound or drive back
down the floor for the game-winning shot? If that's true, then
you and your teams won't win many basketball games. And isn't
that what we're all about here, winning? It seems silly to lose
games because you were too tired at the end, doesn't it?" They
all hang their heads, and then give me a soft "Yes, sir." That's

because they have my message. They know what kind of week they're in for. And after that workout they know why.

A basketball player, especially a young player, will never know how much of a factor his physical conditioning plays when it comes to his game until he needs it most—say, it's the last 2 minutes of the most important game of the season, and all of a sudden his legs turn to rubber, his chest catches fire, and his arms feel like two sacks of potatoes dangling alongside his body. I call that a "conditioning attack," which is what players get when they don't complete the kind of conditioning work off the court that pays off on the court. It's the worst feeling a player can have because he realizes that not only is he letting himself down but he's also letting down the team, the coaches, and all the team's supporters, too.

Everybody gets tired; that's natural. In the NBA, nobody plays every minute of every game, but there are some players who come close. Every season, guys like Michael Jordan, Maurice Cheeks, and Moses Malone play more minutes than anybody else in the league. Other guys play a lot of minutes, too, people like Charles Barkley, Larry Bird, Mark Jackson, John Stockton, players who are very important to their teams. I've averaged about 36.8 minutes in 719 regular-season games over my entire career. That's a lot of minutes; I know I have to be in my best condition even before the season starts. That means I have to follow the advice I give to my campers, once they catch their breath.

Here's the trick: Develop a program made up of the kind of activities you like to do. The only way to produce results and get into peak condition is to maintain the program on a consistent basis, even on the days when the body doesn't feel like doing anything—no running, no lifting weights, nothing more strenuous than getting out of bed. And the only way for players to maintain their programs is to build them around the types of workouts they enjoy.

For instance, not everybody enjoys running long distances, although a basketball game can seem like a marathon in the fourth quarter when the game's tight and players on both teams feel like they've been running for about a week. Those players who don't like to run long distances should concentrate on sprints, 100-yard dashes, and 220-yard runs that will increase their lung capacity and build up the cardiovascular system. They should also find another activity to balance the running.

Weight lifting is another activity that will help most players' games, especially guys who play a lot in the trenches underneath the boards. In the NBA, players like Karl Malone, Buck Williams, Michael Cage, and my teammate A. C. Green look as if they've been lifting weights since they were kids. But younger players whose bodies are still growing should be careful in the weight room. Weights are beneficial, but they can be dangerous, too. So I tell my campers not to start lifting weights until they're at least in their teens and not until they've been taught everything about the weight machines at their schools by somebody who knows what he's doing.

Overall, players should do whatever it takes, in terms of conditioning, so that they'll be ready to play all-out and at their peak for as long as the coach wants them on the court, and for an entire season. I hate to take myself out of games because I'm tired, but it happens. What's important is my recovery time. Usually, I don't need more than a minute or two before I'm ready to come right back in. That's because of the conditioning program I created that's worked for me since I came into the league.

I'm a long-distance runner. Every summer when I'm on vacation, I maintain my conditioning program by running along the beach wherever I'm staying. Running in the sand makes me work harder. My legs get stronger, my lungs work at their peak, and my knees don't take a pounding. A basketball player's knees are the most important part of his body. With all the running and jumping that goes on during a game, they take a pounding every time we play. After ten years, my knees are constantly sore; and after almost every game, I have to treat them with ice packs, which ease the pain and decrease the swelling that occurs after a couple of hours of basketball. My knees are the reason I run in the sand.

I know it's hard to imagine somebody my size loping along the beach like a marathoner, but that's what works best for me. I run for miles. It's relaxing, but it's also getting the job done in terms of my conditioning. Sometimes I'll sprint for about 10 seconds, then return to my regular pace. That gives me the feeling of being in a basketball game where the play stops and starts hundreds of times.

After my jog, I run wind sprints because they will give me the sudden bursts of energy and speed I need when it's time to change directions from defense to offense and run the Lakers'

The pain of an injury can be excruciating—
mentally as well as physically.

fast-break. Most times, those first few steps are the difference be-tween us scoring an easy basket or having to back away and set up our half-court offense. If we can get an edge on the defense at the beginning of the fast-break by getting a quick outlet pass and a solid charge up the court, we're gone and, by then, hard to catch. For just a few seconds, everybody's running as hard as he can, but he might have to stop on a dime in order to change directions or take an open shot. Tired bodies can't do that.

Every player has his conditioning nightmares, and I'm no different. Anybody who's played basketball on a team knows about suicide drills. They're a player's worst nightmare. Coaches love them, but that's only because they're usually on the sidelines watching while we're trying to breathe. As much as I hate them, they work.

When I was younger, on days when I was going to go to the playground or gym and play with my friends, I'd show up about 30 minutes early and run five suicide drills. I'd start at one baseline, sprint to the free throw line, turn around and sprint back to the baseline; then I'd sprint to mid court and come back, then to the farthest free throw line and back; and finally, to the other baseline and back. I'd take about a 30-second break in between, then run them all over again. After the fifth one, I'd walk around until I caught my breath. By the time my friends ar-rived, I was not only warmed up but, after a few days of these extra workouts, also was in such good shape that I was able to outlast everybody on the playground. They'd ask me why, but I wouldn't tell them. It was my secret.

During the season, I don't have to do much conditioning. With eighty-two games, half of them on the road all over the country, the starters and the guys who play a lot of minutes like Michael Cooper, Mychal Thompson, and Orlando Woolridge get pretty good workouts. We usually have to worry more about get-ting the right amount of rest rather than maintaining our conditioning.

Still, some of the guys like to pump iron or play one on one on their own. Mychal Thompson loves weight training. Sometimes I think he'd rather be a bodybuilder than a basketball player. It's kind of a release for him, just like playing one on one is a fun way to work on some parts of your game without the pressure of game conditions.

The guys who don't play much are a different matter. They have to stay in shape because, if another player goes down with an injury, the coaches suddenly need someone to step into their role. Now instead of playing 5 or 10 minutes, those players could play as many as 30 minutes in one night. It doesn't make sense to be out of condition when that chance comes along because, if they're not ready, it might not come along again.

The reserves on our 1988–89 team, guys like Mark McNamara, David Rivers, Jeff Lamp, and Tony Campbell, are always looking for health clubs and other places to work out when we're on the road. It's their way of showing that although they might not get a lot of minutes they're not getting discouraged. That's all a part of being a team, especially a winning team.

All of their efforts paid off at the end of last season during the finals when David, Jeff and especially Tony were called upon to play substantial minutes after Byron and I were sidelined with hamstring injuries. Those were tough moments for the guys. After months of playing only a few minutes every night, suddenly they were asked to play major roles in the most important games of the season. To their credit, all of them performed well. David, being a rookie, was especially nervous. Before the third game of the series—the one in which I played only four minutes because my leg was too tight—David was unusually quiet. Pat told him to be ready. He said it quietly, without any fanfare. Everybody knew that we were asking a lot of someone who didn't really have any experience under the heat of such playoff battles, but we also had faith in him. We had drafted David to back me up at point guard, but he hadn't played a lot of minutes during the season. The transition from college basketball to the NBA is very difficult, especially when a player has to try and break into an established, successful team. On most nights, there just wasn't any time for David, but to his credit, he watched and learned and when he was called he was ready. In fact, we called upon him to take the final shot of game three, which would have tied the game and sent it into overtime. Unfortunately, Joe Dumars of the Pistons made probaby the best defensive play I've ever seen. He had left David open because the Pistons didn't believe the play was for him, but when he saw David alone in the corner he took off, then jumped toward David's shooting hand. Then Joe not only blocked the shot, but he caught the ball in midair while he was going out of bounds, spun in the air and passed it to one of his teammates, Bill Laimbeer, before he landed out of bounds. It was unbelievable. It was plays like that which told me that the

Pistons really wanted to be champions. And they were ready to be champions. I just wish it hadn't been at our expense.

Any off-season conditioning program must start gradually. I usually take about the first forty-five days of the summer off completely in order to give my body time to heal from the season and the play-offs and get back to normal. I need that time. Then when I'm ready to begin, I start with runs of one to one-and-one-half miles. That's six laps around a quarter-mile track. For my campers who don't have a track near their homes, I tell them to ask their parents to use the family car to measure three-quarters of a mile on a road near their house that doesn't have a lot of traffic. They can do that on their way to work. You can then run to that spot, turn around, and run home. If their parents don't have a car, I tell the campers to just run at a nice, steady pace until they start to feel tired; then they can turn around and come home. At the end of each week, I tell them to run a little farther than they did the week before, and maybe at a little faster pace. Then they should just keep increasing the distance, and before they know it, they're in the best shape of their lives.

Believe me, no matter what kind of basketball shape anybody's in, they'll feel better almost immediately after they start doing other things to increase their conditioning. There's no better feeling than when the person I'm playing against starts breathing hard and bending over to catch his breath when I feel as if I've just started. I just look at them and smile, right before I drive around them for the winning basket.

Some players don't like any kind of running, sprints, or long distances. But I recommend that players at least try to maintain a routine that includes both types of running—sprinting and long-distance—at least until they find out whether a program that includes either one or the other will work for them.

Swimming is great, too, especially if players are concerned about their legs. And if they really want a workout where they can cover some miles and enjoy the scenery, cycling is the best routine, especially in areas where there's plenty of hills. A cyclist will treat the hills like a fast-break, pumping his legs as fast and as hard as he can until he reaches the peak. It's safe as long as the rider wears a helmet and follows the traffic laws.

Whatever kind of program a player finally decides on, he should make sure it gets him in condition in time for the first practices of the season. A lot of people just play basketball to get into shape, but there are a lot of reasons why that may not be the right strategy.

First, playing basketball is a lot easier when I'm in shape, and I wouldn't want to make it seem like the drudgery of running windsprints. When I'm playing basketball I want to think about the way I'm playing the game, not about whether I'll be sitting on the sidelines, catching my breath. Second, when I'm tired, I can't play at full speed. When I don't play full speed, I'm setting myself up for possible injury. In the NBA, a lot of players get hurt when they're trying to hold back to save themselves for the fourth quarter or when they're just too tired to play as hard as everybody else on the floor. Usually, the coach will take a player out when he's tired. But my attitude is that I worked too hard to earn my playing time just to give it up down the stretch because I wasn't in condition.

If young players carry that kind of attitude into their off-season conditioning program, it'll give them extra incentive on those days when they believe they're too tired to exercise. They may not be as talented as some of their teammates, but toward the end of practices when most of their teammates are dragging, they'll still have something left in reserve. It's at the end of practices when coaches are the most impressed. That's when they look around and see who's still giving 100 percent. I tell my campers to be in such good condition that, when their coaches look around the floor at the end of their practices they'll be the ones running up and down the floor with energy and enthusiasm, rather than huffing, puffing, and wondering why they ever showed up in the first place.

Over the last several seasons, the Lakers have made it a challenge to come into training camp in peak condition. That way we're already ahead of most of the other teams in the league. It also means that we'll have more time to work on playing basketball, we'll probably get off to a faster start when the season begins, and we'll have fewer injuries.

I had worked particularly hard before last season. I took my training program to another level. I added more running and cycling, anything that would help my cardiovascular conditioning. By the time training camp started in October, I thought I was in the best shape of my life. That's why my two hamstring injuries were so frustrating. Sometimes, you can do everything right, but something can still go wrong.

I've played ten seasons and missed only 104 games out of 820 because of injuries, most of them (45) when I hurt my knee in 1981, but even that's misleading. I've actually played in almost 1000 games when you include the play-offs. The Lakers have been fortunate to enjoy a lot of success in the play-offs, but that also means a lot of extra games.

During my career, I've played in 264 play-off games. So you could say that I've really played another three seasons. It's taken its toll. By the end of every season, my entire lower body is sore, while my shoulders and arms are usually bruised and battered, too.

Larry Bird's another player who's put on those extra play-off miles. Near the start of the 1988–89 season, he finally broke down when his feet started to hurt. He was scared, and I know the feeling. The hardest decision for any athlete to make is whether to have surgery because there's always a risk. Chances are the body will recover, but a player never really knows. Larry couldn't decide, so he chose to try and rehabilitate himself during the off season, then come back in 1988–89. It didn't work. He played just six games before the pain in his heels became unbearable. Finally, he had surgery, but he missed the entire season. There was nothing that conditioning could have done for Larry—or my hamstring injuries—but for most other players getting in shape is an insurance policy against pain.

During my second year with the Lakers, I missed forty-five games because of a knee injury that required surgery. I was scared. I had some of the best doctors in the country, and the only thing they could assure me was that they'd do everything possible to make my knee healthy again. But even after surgery and three months of strenuous rehabilitation, I still wondered if I would have the same knee, if I would be the same player. I didn't know if I would be as mobile or as fast. I didn't know if the knee would collapse again after a week, a month, a year, or ten years. It is not a good feeling for any young athlete to experience.

Knee injuries are just plain, old bad luck. You can't do anything about preventing them. I've seen players like my former teammate Mitch Kupchak and opponents like Larry Krwstkowiak, Bernard King, and Danny Manning crumple to the floor with knee injuries when no one touched them. It's as if their knee exploded. The reality of being an athlete is that can happen at any time and without any warning. We all live with that fear and try not to think about it.

Overall, I consider myself lucky. Other than missing more than half of the 1981 season because of my knee injury, the most games I've ever missed in one season is fifteen. That happened three years later. So take away that one nightmarish season, and I've only missed an average of six out of eighty-two games every season. Everybody in the NBA wants to play every night, but I don't think anyone would be unhappy with that kind of survival record. I give credit to the stretching exercises I do every day and, of course, old-fashioned good luck. But no matter how much stretching we do or how dedicated we are to our conditioning programs, none of the veteran NBA players are completely pain-free. By the time I reach the court every night, I try to look and perform as if I'm feeling as healthy and loose as I did when I was a rookie. But the truth is that my bones, joints, and muscles are in pain every day, starting when I wake up in the morning, especially during the season. With nearly twenty years of basketball behind me at various levels, every part of my body hurts. In the NBA, the games are rougher than people sitting in the stands or watching on television think; somewhere along the line, I knew I would have to pay for all that punishment. I'm paying for it now. Maybe I was paying for it in the finals against the Pistons last spring.

In the mornings, my legs are so tight that they start to hurt when I turn to get out of bed. My back's sore, too. And depending on whether I've got any little nicks or bruises, I might hurt anywhere from my neck down to my feet, anywhere. It's a lot different than when I first came into the league. Back then, I thought all you had to do was lace up the shoes and say, "Hey, let's go," even though I'm not a naturally flexible person. That's not how it works in the NBA, as I quickly found out.

All I had to do was look at Cap, Kareem Abdul-Jabbar. (We called him Cap because he was the captain of our team.) I was amazed at the things Kareem could do with his body before practices and games. While I was out there during stretching, but struggling to reach my toes, he was putting his foot behind his head, twisting around like a rubber-band man! It hurt me just watching him get in all those crazy positions. Later, he told me that those exercises were all a part of the yoga regimen that he had been practicing since his days at UCLA and that they were the reason why he had lasted so many years. Actually, Kareem

When ten guys play all out, collisions are inevitable. In the end you just hope that
everyone survives.

was the standard when it came to staying healthy and proving the benefits of proper conditioning. He was a walking miracle. Kareem played *twenty* seasons before he retired at the end of the 1989 season. No other player has ever played more than eighteen seasons, and nobody has played at the level Kareem did for so long. He left basketball as the game's all-time leading scorer with 38,387 points, more than some *teams* have scored. He also led the league in games (1,560), minutes (57,446), blocked shots (3,189), field goals (15,837) and shots (28,309). A lot of people will remember Kareem for his skyhook and all the points he scored; I'll remember him as a great friend and teacher, and for his dedication to conditioning and how it helped him stay so healthy. He never suffered a serious injury, never missed more than seventeen games in any season, and averaged only about eight games missed each year over his entire career. That's incredible, especially because Kareem was a center, the position that always gets pounded and punished from all sides. He always said that there was no secret to his longevity. He always credited his yoga.

To Kareem, stretching was as important as any other part of practice. He was so confident in his system that he didn't even tape his ankles, something every other player in the league does as a way of preventing ankle injuries. But then nobody in the league stretched like he did, and no one could argue with his success.

I don't think there'll ever be another player who plays as long as Kareem. One thing I know for certain, it won't be me. Somebody once asked me if I could picture myself playing as long as Kareem; then they said if I could, it meant that I was only halfway through my career. I said, "Halfway?" That made up my mind right there. As bad as I feel every morning, there's no way I could do it all over again for another ten years. I don't think anybody could. Today's game is so much different than it was when Kareem was a rookie out of UCLA back in '69. Back then, power forwards like Dave DeBuschere of the Knicks were only about 6'–6'', 6'–7'' at best. Now you've got Karl Malone at 6'–9'' and 250 pounds; Kevin McHale at 6'–10'' and 225 pounds; Kevin Willis at 7' and 235 pounds; and my teammate, A. C. Green, at 6'–9'' and 230 pounds. They make players like DeBuschere and Tommy Heinsohn look like guards by today's standards, and they're so big and strong that they make the game murder on your body. Now, even with all the medical advance-

Before every game, Lakers trainer Gary Vitti puts me through a rigorous series of stretching exercises. But as I found out last year, sometimes nothing works.

ments, players break down. It's a grueling existence. I know I'm not the only NBA player who hurts when he gets out of bed in the morning.

I tried some of Kareem's exercises, even though it wasn't easy to start stretching exercises at my late age. In fact, I hurt more *after* some of the exercises than I did before. That's only natural, I later learned. But in the end, they definitely helped. The *first* thing I do every morning now is stretch all the pain of 980 NBA games out of my body. I move everything around to make sure it still works. I get down on the floor and wake up every part of my body, one piece at a time. My legs, my knees, my back, my shoulders, everywhere. That's just to get me jump-started every morning. Before I start practice, before a game, and again after both sessions, I take time to stretch again. It might take less than 10 minutes, but it's the most important 10 minutes of my day. As a youngster, it's easy to ignore the importance of stretching. It's boring, just bending this way and that, back and forth, and holding the position for several seconds. A young body can also take the punishment and bounce back easier. At my summer camps, the kids get up every day free of pain and stiffness. They're all ready and eager to play—at least for the first couple of days. After a few days of my workouts, a lot of kids find out what sore muscles are for the first time in their lives. So from the start, I emphasize the importance of completing a proper stretching routine and tell the campers that stretching will keep them from being sore again, as well as helping prevent injuries. For me, stretching time is also thinking time. I kill the boredom by planning my strategies for the day. I think of the mistakes I made the day before and figure out how I'm going to correct them. If someone had taught me about the importance of stretching, I probably wouldn't be as stiff as I am now, and just maybe the Lakers would have won our third straight championship last spring.

Before you begin playing, follow the stretching routine that follows and you'll be well on your way to better flexibility. Stay in each stretch for at least 10 to 15 seconds, but breathe and increase the stretch in each position. Repeat each exercise four times before moving on to the next position. I promise one thing: You'll feel better in the morning.

Even with all the stretching exercises in the world, there'll be times when your luck just runs out. My first occurrence came in January of 1989 when I was driving through the lane against

Head Rolls

With hands on your hips, tilt your head slowly to the right, roll it down, to the left, roll back, and to the right. Keep your shoulders down. Repeat 4 times.

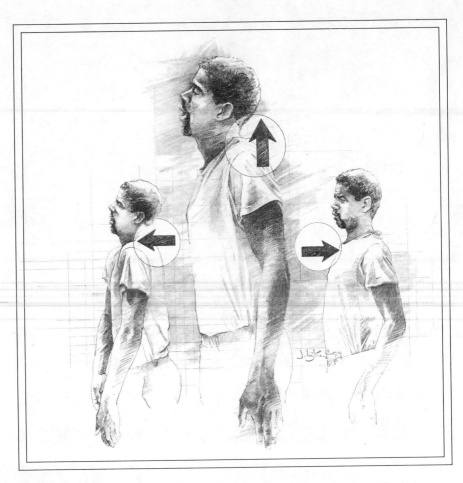

Shoulder Shrugs

With arms down at your sides, lift shoulders straight up, then roll them forward, and then backward. Repeat 4 times each way.

Side Bends

Arms are extended overhead with hands together, shoulders down. Stand erect, then bend to the right, and hold for 10 seconds. Repeat on left side. Bend a total of 3 times each side.

Quadriceps Stretch

Stand erect, holding onto a bar or table edge for balance, if necessary. Bring right leg back and pull foot into body gently with left hand. Hold for 10 seconds. Repeat exercise 4 times each leg.

Hamstring Stretch

Sit on floor with legs together in front of you. Bend forward, reaching as far as you can while keeping knees and back straight. Hold for 10 seconds. Repeat 4 times.

Calf–Achilles Tendon Stretch

Feet shoulder-width apart, stand erect 2 feet from a wall. Move right foot back one step. Place hands against the wall at shoulder height. Lean forward, bending both legs slightly. Push hips forward and slightly down. Keep both heels flat on the floor. Hold for 10 seconds. Repeat 4 times each leg.

Golden State and felt something in my left leg pop. I was trying to get the ball over their center, Manute Bol, who's 7'–6'', and I guess I just reached so quickly that my body wasn't ready for it. I pulled a left hamstring, the same one I would injure four months later in the finals. I tried to keep playing, but I knew I was through for a while. How long? I didn't know. That's the sort of fear every injured athlete feels when he or she suffers an injury. When there's a broken bone or a serious knee injury, it can crush you. The hamstring injury kept me out of the All-Star game in Houston that month, and I missed five games. But because I could walk, I put on my uniform and sat on the bench with the team when they played at the Forum—just like I did in the finals. I figured if I couldn't be out on the floor, the least I could do was provide some moral support. So I cheered and coached as hard as Pat Riley. I don't know if he appreciated it, but he knew I was only trying to help. It was still difficult because I love to play so much. I love being out there. Sitting on the sidelines, I felt empty. I was a cheerleader, but I didn't feel part of the team because that wasn't the role I was used to playing. So what I did away from the arena was pour all that frustration into my rehabilitation. When they wanted me to work out in the morning, I did; but when they weren't looking, I worked out again at night. I was on the weights and the bicycle in the mornings and on the bicycle again at night. All the while, I was hoping that the more I worked out the sooner I'd get back.

I don't know if more stretching could have prevented my two hamstring injuries last year, but I know it didn't hurt me at all. I'd like to play all eighty-two games every season, but that's almost impossible these days. Every season, only about forty NBA players are healthy enough to play in every game. And you can just about count on those teams with healthiest rosters having the best records. Injuries kill a team, whether it's during the regular season when players and coaches are trying to establish a consistency with their roles and substitutions or during the play-offs when the loss of one player can mean the difference between first-round elimination and the championship.

When a player misses a game, especially when he misses a lot of games, it changes everything about his team. Once players on a team get to know each other, everybody plays a particular role. They'd like to play that same role every night. When each player knows what's expected of him, it doesn't leave any room for the kind of petty disputes that usually lead to jealousy and fighting. So when an injury sidelines one player, everybody else's role changes. Everything goes out of whack, and a team will usually start struggling just to survive. The injured player doesn't have to be a starter, either, for it to really hurt your team.

On February 18, 1988, the Lakers lost our best reserve when Michael Cooper went down with an ankle injury. Coop is one of the best sixth man in the league. He's also one of the most durable players in the league. As skinny as Coop is, I used to think he would get murdered out there. But he was out there every night. Starting back in 1982 and going until the injury, Coop missed only 1 game. *One!* That was 1 of 464 games, 565 if you count the play-offs. Coop being hurt was something I couldn't even imagine. Every night he was there. He backs me up at point guard, but he can also play alongside me at shooting guard, where Byron Scott usually starts for us. Coop finishes the break better than anyone on the team, except maybe James Worthy and *nobody's* better than James. Coop's also one of our best jumpers, so we run an alley-oop play called the "Coop-a-Loop." And he's one of the best shooters on the team from 3-point range. Defenses would get so caught up trying to guard Kareem, James, and me that they'd forget all about Coop. He'd be standing out there behind the 3-point circle all by himself; so we'd get him the ball and—bam!—Coop would nail a 3-pointer that would be like a knife in the other team's heart. The Lakers realized how valuable Coop was, but we didn't really know until he went down.

We won nine out of the first ten games without Coop, mostly with the help of adrenaline because we knew everybody had to help take up the slack. Teams will do that. They'll get all fired up when a guy goes down, but it eventually catches up with them. That's what happened to us. Coop missed twenty games because of the injury and wasn't the same for the rest of the season. After that early spurt, we went 13–10 until the start of the play-offs. We won the championship. In the final three rounds we beat Utah, Dallas, and Detroit in three straight seven-game series for our second straight title. But without Coop being completely healthy, we weren't ourselves.

Another factor in conditioning is nutrition. When I was a rookie, I had no standards when it came to my diet. I grew up in a meat-and-potato family, so I thought I could eat anything. I was like most of the other younger players on the team who never considered the connection between what we ate and the overall health of our bodies. To us, watching our diets meant looking for the nearest fast-food place.

Nutrition, eating well, and taking vitamins wasn't as important to most NBA players as it is now. There was a time when everybody saved as much of their daily meal money—$50—as they could. OK, so we were cheap. In terms of food, cheap means a lot of things that aren't really good for your system, like fats, oils, and lots of fried foods. But back then, the greasier the french fries, the better.

But before long, I started to pay for my bad habits. Now almost all professional athletes are concerned about diet and nutrition, not because they necessarily want to keep their weight down but to stay healthy. What you eat makes a lot of difference in terms of your overall health, and it helps us to compete longer. We know that we have to take care of our bodies; our bodies endure so much stress, punishment, and pounding that we need them to take care of us and they must be strong enough to help.

Now I make an effort not to eat red meat because it stays in my system too long. With all the traveling we do during the regular season and the play-offs, our bodies go through difficult adjustment periods every week. Heavy foods only hurt us and keep us from performing at our peak. Of course, there are always temptations. Sometimes I find myself with a meat-and-potato taste, even though I know I'll regret it later. But there's one time when I can't avoid eating more food than I know is good for me—when I go home.

Whenever the Lakers play the Pistons, my mom in East Lansing either has the whole team over for dinner at the house or brings food to the arena. The food fills two or three tables in the locker room. There's usually fried chicken, potato salad, collard greens, cornbread, sweet potatoes, ham, and more desserts than there should be in any one place—other than a bakery—at any one time. It's a wonder we win any games at all when we play in Detroit because we're stuffed with food or looking forward to the goodies waiting for us after the game.

Some guys can eat heavy meals without it weighing them down, but that's what it does to me. I stick with chicken or fish served in a variety of ways, except fried. When I finally gave up red meat on a regular basis about five years after I came into the league, I found myself feeling stronger and knowing I could get in even better condition because I could go harder during my training program. It made a big difference, especially as I got older. It never hurts to get a head start.

Vitamins are also an essential part of my conditioning program. Again, that's something I learned later in life. When I was growing up, I was probably just like you. I didn't want to take my vitamins even though my mom had them ready for me every day. I couldn't see the point. I was young and healthy, and I thought I would be like that forever. Not true. In the NBA, we run so much and lose so much energy and weight every night that we can't afford to think that our bodies will rejuvenate themselves without vitamins. That's the approach every athlete should take, from the guy who plays in a weekend league to the college all-Americans. I tell my campers to ask their doctors to recommend a good multiple vitamin that will suit their bodies' needs—then stay away from fast foods.

**When I'm on the court, I shut off everybody
around me and just play "my game."**

14

The Inner Game

As fans and young players begin to enjoy watching NBA games from the same perspective as the players, they should remember that there are so many inner games taking place inside the team-against-team game that it's almost like a five-ring circus out on the floor! I say five rings because there are five one-on-one match-ups going on all the time, and every pair of opponents usually has its own little mental game going on the side between the two players within the whole game. For instance, take whenever the Lakers play the Celtics. During those games, everybody knows that I always have one eye on Larry Bird and that he always has one eye on me. That's our little game. It's also smart basketball because, when each of us is on the floor, the teams run everything through us; it's smart basketball to keep an eye on the guy who controls the action. But it's more than that. Larry and I *are* almost connected as players. Our personal rivalry within the Lakers–Celtics' rivalry is something that will always mean a lot to me; besides my father's motivation and personal motivation, Larry has always given me something else to strive for and exceed: excellence. When we've beaten a Larry Bird team, the Lakers know we've beaten the best. That's why I really hope the Lakers and Celtics meet in the NBA finals one more time before Larry and I retire. It could happen, even though we lost Kareem after the 1988–89 season and the Celtics had their worst season since Larry came into the league ten years ago. And believe me, it'll be two teams playing with more intensity than you've ever seen before. They'll call it, "For Old Times' Sake."

When I'm not watching Larry during a Celtics–Lakers' game, I even find myself catching a glimpse of James Worthy and Kevin McHale as they go at each other. Kevin is one of the league's best defensive players, and he uses those long arms of his trying to stop James's quickness. I couldn't help but peek at Danny Ainge and Byron Scott, either, before Danny was traded to Sacramento in February 1989. Danny had a lot of confidence; playing against him, especially in Boston Garden, was tough for Byron, so I had to try and keep his spirits up. Robert Parish and Kareem tangled with each other so hard that you couldn't help but take a picture in your mind and put it in your scrapbook. Here were two guys with so much pride battling it out down low where it's always rough. Parish always had his stone face even tighter when he played against Kareem, and Kareem's goggles were almost steaming. They were as intense about each other as they were about the games, and they were as intense about the games as *anybody*. Those are the *inner games* of which fans aren't always aware, but sometimes they're the best games on the floor.

In Chicago Michael Jordan plays his own game, one-against-the-world. A television announcer called him the "best player from another planet." He's so good that it seems he can do almost anything he wants on the court. Michael plays against the *game* every night, rather than a particular opponent. He does his homework on most ends of the floor. He studies the players who defend him, and he breaks down their weaknesses so well that, by the third or fourth time most guys guard him, they're looking at about 50 points on the scoreboard. And he's just as successful on defense. Because he's so strong, he's able to make steals out of plays where someone else might just barely touch the ball or miss it completely.

In 1988 Michael was named Most Valuable Player *and* Defensive Player, the first time that one player won both awards. Then the next season, he took his game even higher. For the last two months of 1988–89, Michael played point guard for the Bulls and put together a string of triple-doubles that even made me jealous. The in the play-offs he started terrorizing teams. He was playing mind games on people from the moment he stepped onto the floor until after the final buzzer sounded, and winning most of them, too. His last-second shot in game five against Cleveland that eliminated the Cavs was one of the most exciting plays I've ever watched. On the second round, he sent the Knicks home with two free throws at the end of game six. In game three of the Eastern conference finals against Detroit, Michael tortured the Pistons for 46 points and hit the game winner with just 4 seconds on the clock, even though he was being guarded by Dennis Rodman who's probably the best defensive player in the league (along with Coop, of course) and Isiah.

But the Pistons are one of the best defensive teams in the league and during the play-offs they were tougher than ever. They were holding teams under 1-0 points on a regular basis, something that's not easy to do during the season, and even more difficult during the play-offs when teams are concentrating even more. But somehow, the Pistons found a way to stop Michael. Maybe he just ran out of gas. I don't know. But they smothered him in the final three games of the series and eliminated the Bulls in six games. Still, Michael was one heck of a one-man show.

I won MVP for the regular season, even though a lot of people said Michael was now the best player in the league. All I know is that when Larry gets healthy, it'll be one great race.

The average fan might not tend to watch the inner game that goes on between certain players. For about three or four trips down the floor, just watch two power forwards like Buck Williams and Charles Oakley go at each other. Man, talk about intensity! They're both about 6'–8'' and all muscles, and they're two of the best in the game. Watching those guys makes me glad I play guard. It's amazing either one of them is standing at the end of the game. Or watch two guards like Dale Ellis and Rolando Blackman. It's like a shoot-out at the OK Corral between those two guys. Or watch two centers like Moses and Akeem; you know they're going all out every play when the other guy is on the floor. Just watch their body language—the bumping and shoving, even when the ball's on the other side of the floor. What you might not see is that they are usually talking to each other, too. One will tell the other, ''Get off me.'' Then the other will respond, ''No, no. You're mine, baby,'' things like that. It's the same thing when two forwards like Adrian Dantley and Mark Aguirre go at each other, especially now that they were traded for each other in the 1988–89 season. A. D. was one of the main reasons why the Pistons were able to take us to seven games in the 1988 finals. He was almost unstoppable in the low post. He's got the game down to a science; no matter what you do to try to counter his moves, it seems as if he's going to find a new move that you haven't even thought of. But Detroit was looking toward the future. Mark is three years younger than A. D., so the Pistons sent Dantley to Dallas for Aguirre, one of my best friends, just like Isiah Thomas. Talk about inner games! Aguirre's presence allowed the Pistons the freedom to spread their offense around, and that was one of the differences in the finals. As for Mark, Isiah and I, we had to put our friendship aside for two weeks and treat each other like mortal enemies during the championship series.

Even when I'm playing, I sometimes find myself watching certain guys go at each other because I know it's going to get heated. Being so close to the action, even if I'm on the bench, I can see their expressions and hear what they're saying; I know it's going to get emotional. I even start doing a little cheerleading if the battle really starts to get good. When Moses Malone and Kareem went at each other during the 1983 championship series, when Moses was with the Philadelphia 76ers and Kareem was still our main weapon, I'd come down the floor and start egging them on like a little troublemaker. Instead of calling a particular play, I'd just say, "Come on Cap, your turn," or "Time to bust 'em Cap." Kareem got into it, too. Everybody was into it. Watching those two great centers was one of the best confrontations I ever saw in the championships.

Most of the time, players play their own little games, even though no one else will know that anything unusual is going on. Sometimes, when Byron comes down and dunks on somebody who's been really physical against him all night, he'll land on the floor and just stare at the man. When Michael Cooper blocks a player's shot, he'll just start talking to the poor guy. He'll start screaming, "Whatchu doin'? Keep that weak stuff outta here!" Then he'll turn to me and start talking to me using the nickname I've had since I was a rookie, Buck. "Man, Buck, can you believe that guy? I mean did you see what I did to him? If he tries it again, I *know* he's crazy." That's Coop. Those are the inner games, the little private wars going on. When Coop and Larry Bird go at it, it's as if there isn't anyone else on the floor. They'll talk up a storm; talking trash is more like it. Bird will come down, bury a jump shot, and start screaming to Coop as he's going back down on defense, "You can't guard me! You know you can't!" Then as they're running down the floor, Coop'll talk back: "You won't get the next one, baby! That last one was just luck." They never stop. But, remember, they're still doing it within the game.

Generally, the Lakers aren't a trash-talking team. Coop talks a lot because that's what fires him up and makes him play better. So we encourage him to talk. But mostly, the Lakers are a *staring* team, especially the later it gets in the play-offs. We want the other team to know that we enjoy taking it to them. It's all about respect, and you go out there trying to earn it. Besides trying to help the team win, players have their personal pride on the line. But I won't ever let my personal pride become more important than the team. If I get too wrapped up in being emotional or trying to play "payback" against some guy who's been defending me, it'll take away from my running the plays correctly or executing the team's defensive rotations; that just defeats the whole purpose of playing: winning.

Most of the inner games at the NBA level are even more intense because most professional basketball players know each other as people probably better than the athletes in any other sport. We've been playing against each other since high school when most of us played in the high school all-star games that take place around the country. Some players have known each other and been playing against each other even longer than that.

Players who grew up in or near big cities like Detroit, Chicago, New York, and Los Angeles have probably known each other since they met in a playground in elementary and junior high school. Isiah and I only heard about each other in high school. He grew up in Chicago and was two years behind me. We never played against each other until we got to the pros. We became friends almost immediately because we shared a lot of the same experiences growing up. In Chicago Isiah grew up in a neighborhood that was much tougher than mine. But like me, he enjoyed the protection of older brothers and sisters, which probably saved him from some of the pitfalls of the streets. The more we talked, the more we realized how much alike we were, how many secrets we shared. That's why meeting in the finals in '88 and '89 was so difficult for both of us. Here we were the best of friends, but we were enemies for two weeks. When the Pistons come to Los Angeles, Isiah usually stays at my house. I have a room upstairs just for him; I even call it Isiah's room. But during the two series with so much on the line, we both decided it would be best if we stayed apart. But we wanted to show each other that, no matter what happened, we'd still be friends and

We can be competitors, and friends, too.

that, once the ball went up, it was war. So when the two teams took the floor for game one in '88, we came out to center court and pecked each other on the cheek. To us it was two friends acknowledging our friendship. Then we acknowledged our respect for the game by the way we played. The following year, we did the same thing. So did Mark and I.

My job was to go out there and play as hard as I could, friendship or no friendship; so, in '88, when I elbowed Isiah as he drove the lane, he knew I was coming. That's why he drove; he knew I was after him. It was just that way. To me it was just a love tap. Isiah's very competitive, just as I am. He knows I let nobody get away with anything. It's just our way. By the end of the play-offs, everyone was making a big deal out of our kiss. We didn't care. It was Isiah, Mark and me expressing our friendship, and we weren't afraid to do that in front of the world.

My relationship with Larry Bird is even stronger than my relationship with Isiah. We have a mutual respect for each other's skills and are great friends. To tell the truth, it seemed that there were so many important games between the Lakers and the Celtics that our relationship came full circle.

We both came into the league in 1979, so early in our careers that we almost hated each other mainly because we were always being pitted against one another. If Larry accomplished something on the floor, everybody wanted to know why I couldn't accomplish it, too. Then if I did something, people bothered Larry about the same thing. Here we were thousands of miles apart on completely different coasts, and we were always having to answer questions about each other. Do you think you're better than Larry? Do you think you're better than Magic? It was crazy. So it wasn't a surprise that when the two teams met twice a year it was really intense regular-season basketball. Reporters from all over the country came to the games, and they all asked the same questions. They'd ask me, "What do you think of Larry?" Then they'd run to Larry and say, "What do you think of Magic?" It got on our nerves, and because we didn't know each other, there was a little resentment between us. But as the years went on, we began to develop more of a friendship. Now we know we have the best rivalry in sports. We also have the ultimate respect for each other, which means we can battle each other in the court and keep it clean. The Lakers used to think of the Celtics as cheap-shot artists, and we found ourselves thinking about nothing but retaliation. It went back and forth between us

When guys like Larry Bird and Kevin McHale
join me for my charity game, it shows that
we all care about supporting a worthy
cause.

Remember, fellas, it's just us against them.

for a lot of years because both teams were trying to establish themselves as the very best in the game. If they took one of our men out, such as they did to Kurt Rambis in the finals in 1984, then we'd take out one of their men. It got very dangerous, and it wasn't basketball anymore. Now we've grown above that, and the two teams just play hard, as hard as we can when we face each other. Playing hard is the ultimate respect.

There's so much pride out on the floor and so much history between the players that the inner games are as crucial as the total game, if not more. But we try not to forget that winning is the ultimate game. I always tell my campers not to let the inner games cause them to lose sight of the whole game, either. This is my advice: If your man outscores you and tries to rub it in your face after your team has won the game, just do what I do. Just point to the scoreboard and smile.

Winnin'—that's what it's all about.

15

Winnin' Time:
The Will to Win

T he mood in the Lakers' locker room during the play-offs is different than it is during the regular season, especially in the championship series. I can feel the difference when I walk through the door. Everybody's there early because they just can't sit around the house anymore. Everybody's antsy, anxious to play. You don't want to do anything else, not even talk to your family.

The two weeks of the NBA finals are the hardest two weeks of my life because all my energy is focused on winning the championship, the ring. My mind, my body, everything's so focused on what's going on that I'd rather be in the locker room with my teammates than anywhere else in the world.

As soon as I hit the locker room, I can feel everybody coming together and becoming more intense. There's no laughing and joking like during the regular season. Then when I hit the floor for warm-ups, I can even feel that the crowd is more intense. They're there for the experience, and they're as serious as the players. It's as if everybody's in this thing together, as if everybody in America is focused on the championship. Then when it's over, win or lose, you're drained.

When we won the championship in 1980, at the end of my rookie year, I really didn't realize what I was going through. I really didn't understand what we had done. The year before

I had won the NCAA title at Michigan State. Two years before that, my high school team won the Michigan state championship. So to me, this was just another championship. I asked everybody, "What's the big deal? We can do this every year!"

It was the next year before I finally understood. We lost in the first round of the play-offs in a best two-out-of-three series against Houston, when I missed a shot at the buzzer by about 2 feet. Just like that, we went from being way, way up to way, way down. Losing that year made me realize the special value of being champions. It made me realize what it took to get there, especially the hard work, concentration, and discipline. I had to realize that as good as it's going now, it can be over just like that.

When people ask me if there's one key ingredient to success in basketball, I always smile and think back to the spring of 1988 when the Pistons took a 3–2 lead against the Lakers in the championship series, and the two teams were headed back to Los Angeles to close out the series—one way or the other. In the Pistons' locker room at the Silverdome in Pontiac, after game five, Isiah told reporters covering the series that after many years in the league he finally discovered what he called the little "secret" that Larry Bird and I had kept to ourselves throughout most of the 1980s when the Celtics and Lakers won eight NBA championships between them in nine years. Now, he and his teammates are part of the inner circle, too. But, truthfully, it's no secret. There's no magic potion that the Lakers, Celtics, Pistons, and Philadelphia 76ers, who won one title during the decade, were too stingy to share. The ingredients to the NBA championship are right there for every player, coach, and team to grab if they can. But it takes time—time, experience, and the will to win.

When I'm playing basketball, I'm playing to win, nothing else. Not to score, to rebound, or to excel in one particular area of the game, but to win. That means I'm a rebounder, a scorer, a passer, even a cheerleader.

It means I'm going to be an example to my teammates of what having a winning attitude is all about.

It means I'll have a burning desire to be the very best player on the best team.

It means I'll have an attitude of unselfishness that keeps me craving for more of the rewards of success, more championships for my team, not glory for myself.

*This MVP trophy may have my name on it,
but I owe it to my father, Earvin, Sr.*

It means I won't ever get jealous of the attention one of my teammates is getting because nobody gets any attention when you lose.

It means I'll set an example at every practice by practicing longer and harder than anybody else.

It means I'll never ask the coach how long we're going to practice, and I'll never worry about how long the team was on the floor. If someone asks me how long I practiced, I'll just say, "I don't know how long. I just played until I finished what I had to do."

It means I'll listen to the coaches and follow their instructions down to the last detail.

It means I'll be an intense competitor who plays fair and respects everybody on the floor—my teammates, the opposition, the coaches, the refs, and the fans—but hates to lose.

It means I'll challenge myself. I'll set goals.

It means I'll do whatever it takes to win.

It means I'll never think that there's something I can't do, whether it's beating my opponent one on one or practicing another hour because something about my game is just not right. But it also means I'll know my limitations and stay within the role the coaches have designed for me.

It means I'll play the inner game within myself, not against someone else.

It means I'll think about "we," not "me," every time I step onto the court.

It means that if the team wins, we win. Winners don't accept excuses and don't make excuses. If I messed up, I'll be the first person to say so.

It means I'll be honest with myself.

It also means *not* using drugs. I'll be high on myself. I'll get high on basketball. We've all been blessed to be able to wake up every morning. And to me, that's Magic.

*Out of my way, I'm taking it home—head up,
legs driving, and with the help of a screen
from my teammate.*

EARVIN JOHNSON, JR. (MAGIC)

Born August 14, 1958, at Lansing, Michigan   **Height 6'-9"**   **Weight 226**
High School—Lansing, Michigan, Everett
College—Michigan State University, East Lansing, Michigan
Drafted by Los Angeles on first round as an undergraduate, 1979 (1st pick)

Collegiate Record

Year	G.	Min.	FGA	FGM	Pct.	FTA	FTM	Pct.	Reb.	Pts.	Avg.
77–78	30	—	382	175	.458	205	161	.785	237	511	17.0
78–79	32	1159	370	173	.468	240	202	.842	234	548	17.1
TOTALS	62	—	752	348	.463	445	363	.816	471	1059	17.1

NBA Regular-Season Record

Season—Team	G.	Min.	FGA	FGM	Pct.	FTA	FTM	Pct.	Off.	Def.	Tot.	Ast.	PF	Dq.	Stl.	Blk.	Pts.	Avg.
79–80—L.A. Lakers	77	2795	949	503	.530	462	374	.810	166	430	596	563	218	1	187	41	1387	18.0
80–81—L.A. Lakers	37	1371	587	312	.532	225	171	.760	101	219	320	317	100	0	127	27	798	21.6
81–82—L.A. Lakers	78	2991	1036	556	.537	433	329	.760	252	499	751	743	223	1	208	34	1447	18.6
82–83—L.A. Lakers	79	2907	933	511	.548	380	304	.800	214	469	683	829	200	1	176	47	1326	16.8
83–84—L.A. Lakers	67	2567	780	441	.565	358	290	.810	99	392	491	875	169	1	150	49	1178	17.6
84–85—L.A. Lakers	77	2781	899	504	.561	464	391	.843	90	386	476	968	155	0	113	25	1406	18.3
85–86—L.A. Lakers	72	2578	918	483	.526	434	378	.871	85	341	426	907	133	0	113	16	1354	18.8
86–87—L.A. Lakers	80	2904	1308	683	.522	631	535	.848	122	382	504	977	168	0	138	36	1909	23.9
87–88—L.A. Lakers	72	2637	996	490	.492	489	417	.853	88	361	449	858	147	0	114	13	1408	19.6
88–89—L.A. Lakers	77	2886	1137	579	.509	563	513	.910	111	496	607	988	172	0	138	22	1730	22.5
TOTALS	716	26417	9543	5062	.530	4439	3702	.834	1328	3975	5303	8025	1685	4	1464	310	13943	19.5

Three-Point Field Goals: 1979–80, 7-for-31 (.226). 1980–81, 3-for-17 (.176). 1981–82, 6-for-29 (.207). 1982–83, 0-for-21. 1983–84, 6-for-29 (.207). 1984–85, 7-for-37 (.189). 1985–86, 10-for-43 (.233). 1986–87, 8-for-39 (.205). 1987–88, 11-for-56 (.196). 1988–89, 59-for-188 (.314). Totals, 117-for-490 (.239).

NBA Play-Off Record

Season—Team	G.	Min.	FGA	FGM	Pct.	FTA	FTM	Pct.	—Rebounds— Off.	Def.	Tot.	Ast.	PF	Dq.	Stl.	Blk.	Pts.	Avg.
79–80—L.A. Lakers	16	658	199	103	.518	106	85	.802	52	116	168	151	47	1	49	6	293	18.3
80–81—L.A. Lakers	3	127	49	19	.388	20	13	.650	8	33	41	21	14	1	8	3	51	17.0
81–82—L.A. Lakers	14	562	157	83	.529	93	77	.828	54	104	158	130	50	0	40	3	243	17.4
82–83—L.A. Lakers	15	643	206	100	.485	81	68	.840	51	77	128	192	49	0	34	12	268	17.9
83–84—L.A. Lakers	21	837	274	151	.551	100	80	.800	26	113	139	284	71	0	42	20	382	18.2
84–85—L.A. Lakers	19	687	226	116	.513	118	100	.847	19	115	134	289	48	0	32	4	333	17.5
85–86—L.A. Lakers	14	541	205	110	.537	107	82	.766	21	79	100	211	43	0	27	1	302	21.6
86–87—L.A. Lakers	18	666	271	146	.539	118	98	.831	28	111	139	219	37	0	31	7	392	21.8
87–88—L.A. Lakers	24	965	329	169	.514	155	132	.852	32	98	130	303	61	0	34	4	477	19.9
88–89—L.A. Lakers	14	518	174	85	.489	86	78	907	15	68	83	165	30	1	27	3	258	18.4
TOTALS	158	6204	2090	1082	.518	984	813	.826	306	914	1220	1965	450	3	324	63	2999	19.0

Three-Point Field Goals: 1979–80, 2-for-80 (.250). 1981–82, 0-for-4. 1982–83, 0-for-11. 1983–84, 0-for-7. 1984–85, 1-for-7 (.143). 1985–86, 0-for-11. 1986–87, 2-for-10 (.200). 1987–88, 7-for-14 (.500). Totals, 12-for-72 (.167).

NBA All-Star Game Record

Season—Team	Min	FGA	FGM	Pct	FTA	FTM	Pct.	—Rebounds— Off.	Def.	Tot.	Ast.	PF	Dq.	Stl.	Blk.	Pts.
1980—L.A. Lakers	24	8	5	.625	2	2	1.000	2	0	2	4	3	0	3	2	12
1982—L.A. Lakers	23	9	5	.556	7	6	.857	3	1	4	7	5	0	0	0	16
1983—L.A. Lakers	33	16	7	.438	4	3	.750	3	2	5	16	2	0	5	0	17
1984—L.A. Lakers	37	13	6	.462	2	2	1.000	4	5	9	22	3	0	3	2	15
1985—L.A. Lakers	31	14	7	.500	8	7	.875	2	3	5	15	2	0	1	0	21
1986—L.A. Lakers	28	3	1	.333	4	4	1.000	0	4	4	15	4	0	1	0	6
1987—L.A. Lakers	34	10	4	.400	2	1	.500	1	6	7	13	2	0	4	0	9
1988—L.A. Lakers	39	15	4	.267	9	9	1.000	1	5	6	19	2	0	2	2	17
88–89—L.A. Lakers	DNP-Injured															
TOTALS	249	88	39	.443	38	34	.895	16	26	42	111	23	0	19	6	113

Three-Point Field Goals: 1980, 0-for-1. 1983, 0-for-2. 1984, 1-for-3 (.333). 1986, 0-for-1. 1988, 0-for-1. Totals, 1-for-7 (.143).

NBA Most Valuable Player, 1987. . . . Named to All-NBA First Team, 1983, 1984, 1985, 1986, 1987, 1988. . . . All-NBA Second Team, 1982. . . . NBA All-Rookie Team, 1980. . . . NBA Playoff MVP, 1980, 1982, 1987. . . . Recipient of Schick Pivotal Player Award, 1984. . . . Member of NBA championship teams, 1981, 1982, 1985, 1987, 1988. . . . Holds all-time NBA playoff record for most assists. . . . Holds NBA playoff game record for most assists, 24, vs. Phoenix, May 15, 1984, and most assists in one half, 15, vs. Portland, May 3, 1985. . . . Holds NBA championship series game records for most assists, 21, vs. Boston, June 3, 1984, most assists in one half, 14, vs. Detroit, June 19, 1988, and shares record for most assists in one quarter, 8, vs. Boston, June 3, 1984. . . . Holds NBA All-Star Game records for career assists and assists in one game, 22, 1984. . . . Led NBA in steals, 1981 and 1982. . . . Led NBA in assists, 1983, 1984, 1986, 1987. . . . Named to *The Sporting News* All-America First Team, 1979. . . . NCAA Division I Tournament Most Outstanding Player, 1979. . . . Member of NCAA championship team, 1979. . . .